SAMS Teach Yourself Today

e-Banking

e-Banking

Managing your money and transactions online

Mary Dixon
Brian Nixon

SAMS

201 West 103rd Street, Indianapolis, Indiana 46290

Sams Teach Yourself e-Banking Today

Copyright ©2000 by Sams Publishing

All rights reserved. No part of this book shall be reproduced, stored in a retrieval system, or transmitted by any means, electronic, mechanical, photocopying, recording, or otherwise, without written permission from the publisher. No patent liability is assumed with respect to the use of the information contained herein. Although every precaution has been taken in the preparation of this book, the publisher and author assume no responsibility for errors or omissions. Nor is any liability assumed for damages resulting from the use of the information contained herein.

International Standard Book Number: 0-672-31882-2

Library of Congress Catalog Card Number: 99-69443

Printed in the United States of America

First Printing: February, 2000

03   02   01   00
4   3   2   1

Trademarks

All terms mentioned in this book that are known to be trademarks or service marks have been appropriately capitalized. Sams cannot attest to the accuracy of this information. Use of a term in this book should not be regarded as affecting the validity of any trademark or service mark.

Warning and Disclaimer

Every effort has been made to make this book as complete and as accurate as possible, but no warranty or fitness is implied. The information provided is on an "as is" basis. The authors and the publisher shall have neither liability nor responsibility to any person or entity with respect to any loss or damages arising from the information contained in this book.

Acquisitions Editor
Jeff Schultz

Development Editor
Alice Martina Smith

Managing Editor
Charlotte Clapp

Project Editor
Andy Beaster

Copy Editor
Patricia Kinyon

Indexer
Greg Pearson

Proofreader
Candice Hightower

Team Coordinator
Amy Patton

Interior Designer
Gary Adair

Cover Designer
Jay Corpus

Copywriter
Eric Borgert

Editorial Assistant
Angela Boley

Dedication

For Arthur Dixon and Arthur Nixon, our great dads.

Table of Contents

Introduction   1

Part I Getting Started

1. The Revolution Is Upon Us   7
2. What Online Banking Means to You   19
3. What You'll Need for Online Banking   35
4. Choosing Your Bank   47
5. Ready, Set, Stop: Do Your Due Diligence   59

Part II Using Online Banking Products and Services

6. Begin with the Basics: Opening an Account and More   71
7. No Postage Necessary: Paying Bills Online   85
8. Beyond the Basics: Cool Add-On Products and Services   97
9. Shortcuts to the Best Deals   111
10. Attention All Small Business Owners   121

Part III The Facts About Security and Privacy

11. Trust Is More Than a Word   135
12. The Dark Arts: Cryptography and Encryption   147
13. Privacy Please! How to Protect Your Privacy and Who Else Cares About It   159
14. Your Privacy and Security Checklist   173

Part IV The Banking Revolution Is Just Beginning

15	What Customers Like Best About Their Online Banks	183
16	The Bottom Line on Sanity and Banking Online	193
17	Welcome to the Future: What's Next for Online Banking?	205

Part V Appendixes

A	Banking Sites in This Book	215
	Glossary	225
	Index	235

Acknowledgments

A book of this scope is not written and produced in a vacuum by two authors huddled over their keyboards night after night. We want to thank the many sources who contributed their views and shared their expertise on online banking as it currently stands and where it is headed in the future. We also wish to thank the members of the Macmillan publishing team for conceiving of this project and working diligently and efficiently to help us bring it to completion. The Macmillan team contributed to the format and style of this book, which we hope you'll find both useful and helpful. We would also like to note that any sins of omission are ours alone and not those of the excellent Macmillan staff.

INTRODUCTION

Ever get a tour inside your bank? That's what we bring to you in this book. No, not a look at your bank's vault of cash or at the safe deposit box area, but at something valuable nonetheless. We're going to take you inside the world of online banking.

We're able to provide this perspective because we have worked together producing a banking magazine, *Community Banker*, which is published by America's Community Bankers, the Washington, D.C. trade association for community banks. We write about banking all the time. We talk to bankers and their consultants on a daily basis.

Our lives revolve around the interests of our readers who are community bankers across the nation. They compete with mega-institutions such as Citibank and Chase Manhattan. These community banks have been racing to keep up in the technology game, including placing their products and services online.

Throughout 1999, banks have geared up for the year 2000 date change. Regulators were on them to make sure that their systems wouldn't crash on New Year's Day. They spent millions of dollars preparing and preparing. In doing so, many upgraded their computer systems and began gearing up for their next technological challenge—transforming themselves into online banks accessible to their customers from anywhere, at anytime, with a click and the Internet.

As banks move online, there's a definite feeling of "dot-com madness" in the industry. You can't go to a banking industry conference without experiencing a heavy emphasis on e-banking. Banks are speeding ahead to create their online sites for one big reason—they want your business. Many bankers face a definite learning curve about the technology and promise of the Internet, but they are fearful that if they don't get online, their customers will be snatched away by other online banks. They also fear non-

Note:
James Pushnill, an analyst for Forrester Research Inc., a consulting firm following the progress of e-commerce, told us: "Any bank that hasn't moved yet into Internet banking is still stuck in first gear."

banks, such MSN.com and Charles Schwab, who are gradually getting into the banking business.

Online Presence but No Meat:
When we went to press, the Federal Deposit Insurance Corporation was reporting that 30 percent of all banks and thrifts had a Web presence. But only 7 percent had transactional Internet sites where you can actually perform banking functions and not just read marketing materials about an institution.

What does this mean for you? It's a great time to start banking online. The industry has progressed enough to offer you some dynamite, user-friendly sites—and the fees at most of the banks are low. We think it's smart to shop around for a bank that doesn't charge for this service, but then again, your priority might be banking at a site that navigates well. To some of us who are pressed for time, that's just as important as money.

We got hooked on e-banking after we began the practice ourselves. It's convenient, fast, and empowering. The first time you log on to view your account history or to transfer funds, you feel like you won't ever have to stand in another teller line again. And many other functions are available as well, including paying bills, buying checks, getting a loan, or even just checking out the location of the closest branch. You never have to get stuck in telephone darkness again—"Press 1 if…press 2 if…press 3 if…"—where you're left wondering what button to press to speak to a real, human person.

Banks as Starting Point:
Bill O'Connell, vice president of marketing for Home Account (an Internet provider for banks), told us that banks need to think of their sites as "financial service hubs—basically a financial service portal site."

When you bank online, you can perform most banking functions without having to rely on a banker. Many sites are easy to navigate or surf, and they require very little information or keying in of information. You can bank at midnight, in your pajamas, while watching television. You can bank from anywhere in the world, as long as you have an Internet connection.

During our research on the book, we surfed more than 100 banking sites. We quickly learned what the best institutions have, including 24-hour personal service over the telephone. Yes, the sites are easy to navigate, but you will undoubtedly have a question now and then. We say: Insist that your bank provide this 24-hour service.

As you read this book, remember that we have taken a strong consumer angle. We wanted to bring our industry knowledge to the table so that you will be a customer that is not intimidated by any of the growing array of financial services providers, online or offline.

> **Inexpensive and Worth It**
> David Becker, chief executive officer of First Internet Bank of Indiana (*www.firstib*), is convinced that Internet banking is here to stay. He says 40 million Americans will bank online by the end of 2000. As a banker, he likes the fact that it costs an institution $2 for each transaction in a teller line compared to a penny for each online transaction. (In just three months, Becker spent $800,000 marketing his online bank!)

In this book, you will learn the basics—how to chose a bank and how to get started. We will take you through all the prime functions. We venture onto actual Internet bank sites and take you step-by-step through such features as viewing your account, transferring funds, paying bills, and acquiring a loan or credit card. We also show you that not all bank sites are equal. We point out what we like and don't like. You won't need to be online as you read this book—we have captured many screens from the banks' sites so that you can see the result of each click as we describe it.

We spend a lot of time explaining privacy and security issues. Both are a top concern to you and your banker. As we begin to perform much more of our commerce and financial services functions online, it's imperative to understand these issues and to take steps to help ensure the safety of your information and money as it travels across the expansive Internet world.

In addition, we have included throughout the book our special insights into the banking industry. Many of the terms we use and the tips we provide will help you as you bank online or offline.

We'll leave you with one question as you start reading this book:

> Which bank site, Figure 1 or Figure 2, is more convenient, empowering, and will make you feel a part of the new century?

Figure 1: You can walk or drive through the city streets and stand in a teller line for a long time.

Figure 2: You can go onto your bank site, check out your accounts, and pay a few bills. (Citibank estimates this will take you 10 minutes.) And, yes, you can do this anytime, anywhere.

So, how will you bank? In the real world with real-world hassles? Or online in your underwear?

Mary Dixon
New York, N.Y.

Brian Nixon
Washington, D.C.

PART I
Getting Started

CHAPTER 1

The Revolution Is Upon Us

The way we banked growing up in the 1960s is long forgotten today. We would go to banks where our parents opened accounts for us, give our passbooks to a teller, and hand to her $5 in hand-wrapped dimes. She would stamp our books with a date and write in our deposit for the day. We would leave very happy with a sucker in one hand, our passbooks in the other, and hopes of going to college with the money we would save spinning in our heads.

The authors have both gone to college now, eaten a few too many suckers, and instead of keeping track of our money with ink and paper, we do it with clicks of a mouse and digital transmissions. We bank online. We think you should, too.

The financial institutions where we learned the practice of banking online are Citibank (*www.citibank.com*) and Wachovia (*www.wachovia.com*).

What You'll Learn in This Chapter:
- How technology is changing banking.
- The first banks on the Internet.
- Who is banking online.
- Why you should, too.

We don't think these sites are perfect, but they are the banks where we got our start in online banking. Citibank's Direct Access service and Wachovia's redesigned site show some of the best aspects of an online bank.

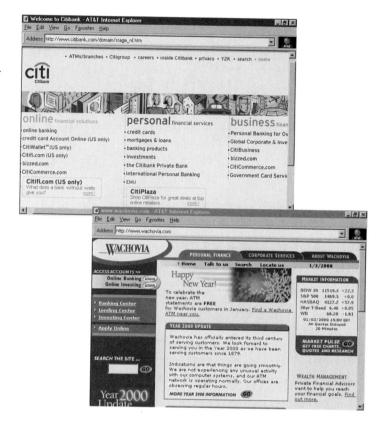

Our Best Tip at Tip-Off

After you find a bank online, how do you know if the site will be user-friendly? The answer lies in the bank's online "demo." We encourage you to click into a bank's demo so that you can test drive the site before signing up. These demos allow you to learn how to view funds, transfer funds between accounts, pay bills, and much more.

Mary has been banking online with Citibank since 1999, and Brian has been with Wachovia since 1998. That doesn't seem like a long time, but in the circle of e-bank customers, we are considered old timers. Take another look at the Wachovia screen. This North Caroline-based institution redesigned its site in 1999 to become more user friendly. Just think how far this bank has come since it was founded in 1879.

Technology Changes Everything

We're not using beads, eggs, feathers, or oxen as money anymore. We've come a long way since pigs and vodka were used as currency. Today, you can be the richest person in your neighborhood and never even touch money. We live in the e-age where wealth is recorded, stored, and transferred around the world in seconds using electrons. Technology is revolutionizing banking, like most everything else, at a rapid pace that's hard to fathom.

What technology is changing the way we bank?

The three technological realities allowing for the development of online banking are the computer, the Internet, and *encryption* and *firewalls* (the development of secure transmitting systems over the expansive, wide-open world of the Internet).

High-tech applications are not new to the banking industry, which has long relied on computers to process checks, run ATMs, store data, transfer funds, process loans, and measure risks. This move into electronic banking is a natural fit for the financial services industry. But experts in the field agree that the move to the Internet is marking a time during which the industry has seen the biggest and most rapid changes in history, driven by new and even more powerful technologies.

> **The Online Requirement**
> Does a bank have to offer e-banking to compete in the new century? Here's what Lynn Busing, executive vice president of CheckFree Corporation, a major player in financial electronic commerce, told us:
> "Historically, banking has been an industry based on customer service. Banks that failed to provide superior service simply vanished. In today's browser-based marketplace, banks need to leverage this customer service philosophy with Web-empowered features for attracting and keeping customers."

Everyone Needs a PC

According to *The Community Banker's Guide to the Internet and Home Banking*, a how-to book for bankers published by America's Community Bankers, U.S. consumers began buying more PCs than television sets in 1994. By 1995, 35 million Americans had computers in their homes.

Forrester, an e-commerce consulting firm, reports that 12.7 percent of U.S. households had computers in 1995. In 1999 alone, Forrester predicted that 13.2 million home computers would be sold in the United States and nearly 4.5 million households would purchase their first computers. Because we all need access to home computers before we can access online banks, this

The History of How the PC Developed:

Apple Computer Incorporated jump-started our love of personal computers in the 1970s with its Apple II and offered us its updated version of the PC in the 1980s with the Macintosh.

In 1981, IBM introduced its first personal computer. In a year and a half, the company sold 136,000 units. Also in 1981, Adam Osborne introduced the first portable computer, the Osborne 1.

In 1982, *Time* magazine named the PC its "Man of the Year."

development was vital. We've come a long way since the first home computer, the Altair, was developed in 1974. The Altair 8800 was sold unassembled by Micro Instrumentation and Telemetry Systems Incorporated. It proved to be popular only with the computer whizzes who had the time and brains to assemble these machines.

The Development of the Internet

The Internet dates back to the 1960s. The builders and inventors of the electronic highway were originally trying to create a system for researchers and the military. As the system grew larger, organizations that wanted to bring standards to the Internet began to develop, including the InterNetworking Group (INWG). The "Father of the Internet," Vinton Cerf, was the first chairman of the INWG in 1972. Twenty-five years later, in 1997, when the Internet became a common form of communication for many of us, President Clinton awarded Cerf and Robert E. Kahn, the U.S. National Medal of Technology for founding this remarkable virtual world.

The 1980s ushered in several years of rapid development of the Internet. The common language for the system (TCP/IP) was created, and corporations began to use it as a way to talk to their customers. This communication can be seen as the dawn of e-commerce. In 1994, Pizza Hut was one of the first corporations to begin selling its products online by accepting orders through cyberspace.

Encryption and Firewalls Mean Security

Throughout the 1990s, the Internet has become more secure because of the development of better encryption. *Encryption* allows users to send messages to specified recipients without others being able to read them. Encryption relies on special instructions that scramble a message so that no one except the intended recipient can read it. Encryption works only if hackers or other electronic thieves haven't gained access to the decoding software.

The military started using encryption first, but now businesses—including banks—use this technology to increase the security of their systems. When a site is encrypted, you, the user, don't have to do anything special with the data coming or going from your computer; the scrambling and descrambling occurs in the background of your computing. Only authorized users are presented with the unscrambled data.

In addition to encryption, banks have developed more sophisticated firewalls to prevent unauthorized access to their systems. *Firewalls* are hardware and software placed between two networks through which all traffic must pass. Firewalls prevent hackers from gaining access through a "back door." For example, firewalls ensure that unauthorized users can't access your banking account over the Internet. Only you, who knows the password to your account, will be granted access to your records.

Banks Jump Online

Banks were soon to follow the pizza maker into the world of e-commerce. As early as the 1980s, banks were offering their customers access to their accounts with their computers—but not over the Internet. Instead, the first computer home banking systems were direct-dial. A customer's computer would connect directly with the bank through a telephone line. For customers to make this connection, they needed their financial institution's proprietary software—which was especially designed to communicate only with that bank's system.

In May 1995, Wells Fargo became the first bank in the world (according to the Online Banking Report) to begin offering customers access to their accounts over the Internet. However, this early system only allowed customers to see, not access, their accounts. Wells Fargo has a come a long way since the days when it transmitted or delivered money in a stage coach. Today, it is a leader in electronic banking.

This is Wells Fargo, first established in 1852, a long, long time ago. In its early days, the company was known for its stage coaches carrying mail and cash across the United States. During the Gold Rush, Wells Fargo was the first bank to initiate an electronic transaction by telegraph in 1864.

This is Wells Fargo today. It offers an online banking site that gets a lot of accolades.

Wells Fargo (*www.wellsfargo.com*) no longer moves at the speed of horses. But rather at the speed of electrons.

Following the May 1995 Wells Fargo milestone on the Internet, Security First Network Bank unveiled a fully-transactional Internet banking site on October 18, 1995. *Fully-transactional* meant that customers could view their accounts, access them, and move money around. Security First Network Bank also holds the honor of being the first FDIC-supervised bank online.

Security First Network Bank, whose home page is shown in the following figure, consistently ranks high in surveys of sites. In 1999, the company began to offer 6 percent interest on checking accounts. It's that type of strategy—offering great deals—that online banks hope to use to take customers away from the old-fashioned brick-and-mortar institutions.

Security First is a tough competitor in the online banking world.

In 1999, Net.B@nk became the first profitable Internet-only bank. At that time, the bank claimed more than 54,000 accounts throughout the United States and in 20 foreign countries. Its attractions include free online account access, free unlimited bill payment, free checks, and free unlimited ATM use. Net.B@nk's home page is shown in the following figure.

Net.B@nk is the first Internet-only bank that has proved to be profitable. With all the free goodies it offers its customers, it's no wonder the site works.

By 1999, more than 5,100 federally-insured depository institutions were online in some way. That's about 24 percent of all banks, savings associations, and credit unions. This number is expected to grow rapidly.

There are basically two reasons why banks are going online: They want to keep up with other banks that are going online, and they want to save money by reducing their expenses of supporting brick-and-mortar branches and employees. According to Booz, Allen & Hamilton, a consulting firm, it costs a bank about $1 to deliver a manual transaction at a branch; by contrast, an ATM transaction costs 25 cents and an online transaction costs a whopping 1 cent.

First Come the Banks, Then Come the Customers

As the number of online banks increases, so do the number of online banking customers. One estimate from International Data Corporation is that households conducting online banking would increase from 6.6 million in 1998 to 32 million by 2003. Jupiter Communications, an e-commerce analyst, has predicted that the number of online banking households will grow from 3.8 million in 1998 to more than 26 million by 2003. Jupiter estimates that will be about 25 percent of all U.S. banking households in that year. Jupiter forecasts that by 2003, 18 million U.S. households will be receiving their bills online.

One demographic that online bank customers have in common is that they are dealing with a nice-size income. Jupiter estimates that 69 percent of online banking households make over $50,000. The firm predicts this will decrease by 2003, when only 59 percent of the online banking households will make more than $50,000. More and more of us are expected to own home computers, understand how e-banking works, and trust the security systems.

Why You Should Join the Online Crowd

Although there are many reasons to bank online, we've narrowed the number down to 10. If you can relate to any of these, go ahead: Begin banking online today.

1. *You never will have to wait in a teller line again*—You simply log on from home or anywhere in the world and access your accounts directly over the Internet. No one is ever ahead of you, slowing you down.

2. *Your bank is never closed*—ATM machines brought us this 24-hour concept, but with Internet banking, you don't even have to leave your home. Yes, although an ATM allows us to get cash at any time, it definitely isn't the best tool to conduct

other banking transactions 24 hours a day. With e-banking, you don't ever have to put yourself at risk of a crime by going to an ATM late at night. When you e-bank from home, you can view your accounts, pay bills, transfer funds, and conduct a long list of other functions at anytime, day or night.

3. *You have direct access to your accounts*—It's a hassle to go to your bank and ask for a printout of your statement in the middle of the month. You don't have to worry about that anymore. You can pull up your balances and view transactions at any time. You can see whether a check has cleared or whether a direct deposit has been placed into your account.

4. *If you have children away at college, you can better manage their school accounts and spending*—Suppose that your son calls one day to say that he just spent his last dollar on school books and is out of money. With e-banking, you can act on this request with more information than your son is willing to give. You go online to view his account, an account to which you also have access, and you see that the ATM debit card was last used in a bar and that the transaction before that was at a record shop. It's not nice to spy, but you can talk to your child and be better informed by having access to the history of how he is spending his money. You can also log on to his account, see that his balance is declining, and transfer funds from your personal checking or savings account into his account if that seems appropriate.

5. *You can bank from anywhere in the world as long as you have access to a computer and the Internet*—If you are a traveler, this comes in handy when you are away from home and need to pay a bill. You simply go to your bank's site, and the bank will either electronically pay the bill or cut a check. Many do this for free.

6. *It won't matter if you run out of checks or stamps*—You find yourself having to pay a few bills one night, but you don't have any checks or stamps (or both). Again, simply pay these bills online. Some banks allow you to pay an unlimited

number of bills each month with no charge. Think about the money you can save in postage!

7. *You can bank conveniently even if you are disabled, sick, or elderly*—If, for some reason, you can't drive to the bank one day, there's no need to worry. You can still do your banking. Simply log on.

8. *You can bank at home even if you're in the military overseas*—If you are stationed away from home for several months, Internet banking allows you to maintain your bank accounts on the home front. Not to mention you can check to make sure that the Army or Navy is depositing your pay every month into your account.

9. *You can get more options and perhaps better deals*—Online banks are competing against each other and the traditional banks for your dollars and business. Internet banking has intensified the competition between banks because geographical barriers have disappeared. You can live in New York and bank with an institution in Atlanta with no trouble. Because customers can shop around now, banks are offering better deals—including higher interest accounts, great rates on certificates of deposits, and no-fee ATM transactions.

10. *You can naturally embrace new technologies*—If you give online banking a try, you will get hooked. It's a kick to view your account balances for the first time without having to visit a bank or an ATM. It's especially thrilling to move your money around in your accounts with a simple click.

Get Your Bank Online

What can you do if you want your bank to offer e-banking services or offer better online features?

Tripp Rackley, chairman and chief executive officer of nFront, a provider of Internet banking systems, told us this: "Consumers can have the most influence when consumers actively use their bank's Internet site for all of the services the bank offers, including bill pay and transactions, and not use the site for simply checking balances. Consumers can also exert significant influence on those banks that are not yet online, first by vocalizing their desire to have access to Internet banking, and if that doesn't work, by voting with their feet and taking their business elsewhere."

What You Should Know Now

After reading this chapter, you should have learned the following:

- Technology has advanced enough to make banking online safe.

- Banking online remains a relatively new adventure for the industry and the consumer, with Wells Fargo leading the way in 1995.

- Online banking is great for the traveler, the student, the parent with children away at school, anyone based overseas, and anyone looking for convenience and a way to bank while sitting at home.

In short, online banking is great for anyone looking for more control of his or her bank accounts.

CHAPTER 2

What Online Banking Means to You

Banks are facing competition from all types of businesses. Department stores, insurance companies, investment firms, and credit card companies are all competing to manage our dollars. Nordstrom, T. Rowe Price, American Express, Aetna, and MSN.com are a few examples of the newest players offering banking services.

Aetna (*www.aetnafinancial.com*) has developed a comprehensive financial services center online. The site features educational materials for planning for the future and offers retirement funds such as IRAs.

MSN.com's MoneyCentral (*http://moneycentral.msn.com/home.asp*) offers an abundance of advice on financial services, and it also features a bill payment function.

Basically, banking is far from what it used to be. More and more companies, even those not traditionally offering financial services, are vying for your money and savings.

In addition to the new businesses entering the market, your community or regional bank has to compete nationally because institutions of all sizes are offering products and services to customers who live just about anywhere in the world and have access to the Internet. Online banking has kicked competition up a notch in the financial services world.

With this intense competition, banks are going online and trying to outdo each other with the services they offer and by mitigating any of the accompanying costs. Banks see their competition coming at them from all directions, so some of the services they are beginning to offer may surprise you.

What You'll Learn in This Chapter:
- What banks offer at their sites.
- A complete review of products and services.
- A few things banks don't want you to know.

Take for instance, the Exchange Bank of Perry, a small bank in Oklahoma. It not only offers you access to your checking account online, but this bank, established in 1896, also tells you what your children will be eating at school for the week. Banks will provide this type of community information to keep you coming back to their sites. In fact, The Exchange Bank of Perry is more than just an online banking site, it serves as an Internet service provider (ISP) to the residents of Perry. That means that the bank itself is the provider of the on-ramp to the information superhighway. Before the bank offered this service, residents of Perry had to dial long-distance to get on the Web.

Most banks think they've done you a service by telling you their interest rates. This small bank in Perry, Oklahoma, goes a step farther and reports that its customers' children will be eating hamburgers, tater tots, ranch beans, and peaches this week.

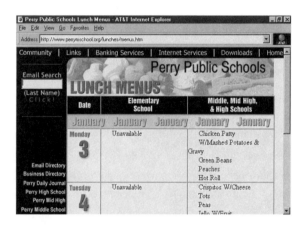

In addition to teaching you about the services you should expect from your online bank, we will give you an insider's view of some of the nuances in online banking that bankers don't exactly highlight for you. We don't think any of these points should stop you from banking online, but we do think that understanding them will make you a better informed consumer.

All Bank Sites Are Not Alike

Not all banks are on the Internet, but if they are, they will provide basically two types of sites. Some have sites that merely tell you what products and services they are offering in their brick-and-mortar branches. Such basic Web sites don't allow you to view your accounts or transact any business. These are called *informational sites* or *static Web pages*. If your bank is merely offering this type of site, you may want to ask your banker to take the next step to *transactional Web banking*, which allows you to do everything that is offered in the institution's branches and more because you have direct control of your accounts.

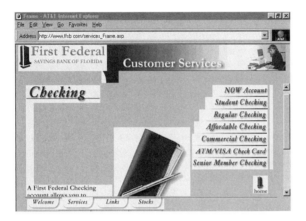

The First Federal Savings Bank of Florida gives out some handy information about their services here, but you can't bank online.

Many sites mark the next generation. You can perform a long list of banking functions at these transactional types of sites. They come in all sizes; some even operate only online, meaning that they have no real, offline branches.

One example of a small local bank going fully online with a transactional site is United Bank in Atmore, Alabama. You can view your accounts, transfer funds, order checks, and manage a few other tasks. When we went to press, the bank didn't yet offer its customers a way to pay bills online—but that feature is coming soon.

United Bank's site has one of the best services we found during our tour of online banks. The bank has a Web page that tells and *shows* you who is in charge of its Internet operation. It also gives you a phone number, so you can call Amy, and an email address, so that you can write to her. If you encounter any problems or have any questions when banking online, this type of information is invaluable.

After viewing hundreds of banking sites while writing this book, we had to show you this screen from United Bank's Web site. It's a prime example of real-world customer service at a virtual bank branch.

Telebank.com is one of the hottest competitors in the online banking world. It offers a complete set of services. This bank has been specializing in alternative delivery since 1989, when it began offering its products and services over the telephone and through the mail. Now it's an Internet player, and its home page is shown in the next figure.

Telebank.com, which made a name as a telephone banking service, is trying to do the same with Internet delivery. Notice how it promotes its competitive rates on its front page. Many Internet banks are hoping that their better rates will convince you to do your business with them.

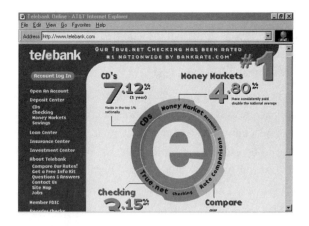

What to Expect at Fully Transactional Sites

The best advice we can give as you get started as an online banking customer is to take it one click at a time. That way, you won't get overwhelmed and will learn to take advantage of all your bank's offerings. Each bank is different, but we've surfed hundreds of sites taking note of what is available. The following sections include some of the more popular products and services offered by online banks.

Account Viewing

Account viewing features allow you to log on to a site and see your account balances or see your recent transactions. For example, you can see what ATM withdrawals or deposits you've made or see what checks have cleared. This is a basic but extremely helpful feature of online banking. After you have registered as a customer, you can immediately begin taking advantage of this service and others. To open an online account, some banks make you go to a physical branch to fill out the paperwork, but others let you do this directly online. At many sites, you can open savings and checking accounts on the spot. Banks will request that you transfer the funds with a credit card or that you mail in your first deposit. So this isn't an instant process, unless you already have funds deposited in the bank.

To see how easy and fun account viewing can be, let's take a tour of Crestar Bank (*www.crestar.com*). Account viewing at most of the bank sites is pretty similar.

1. Log on to the Crestar Bank at *www.crestar.com*. When the home page opens, click the Bank Online link to open that page in the site.

2. Crestar offers a demonstration account that you can play with to determine how easy it is to view and manipulate accounts. From the Bank Online home page, click the Demo link.

3. Here is where you sign on. Notice that it's not that difficult. The bank only wants to know your bank card number and PIN. On this page, you click Sign In to go directly to a page where you can view your account balances.

4. To view a history of the recent transactions in an account, just click the account number (in the first column) that you want to investigate. A new page opens, showing the most recent transactions for that account.

A Love/Hate Relationship:
According to a survey conducted for eFunds, a provider of Internet products for banks, 80 percent of U.S. consumers rate their online banking experience higher than their traditional brick-and-mortar banking ones. The same survey shows that only 13 percent of the online bank consumers do *all* their banking online.

▼ **Try It Yourself**

5. In the initial account viewing page, Crestar allows you to see all the activity in the account since your last statement. Then you can indicate that you want to see other activity. For example, you can get a glimpse at today's transactions or the activity from a prior statement. If you have a question about any of the transactions, you can click an envelope icon next to the notation in question to send an email to the bank with your question.

At the Crestar Bank site, you can view a demonstration account that lets you see how easy it is to log on and view your account balances. If you click one of the accounts, you can review the recent activity in that account.

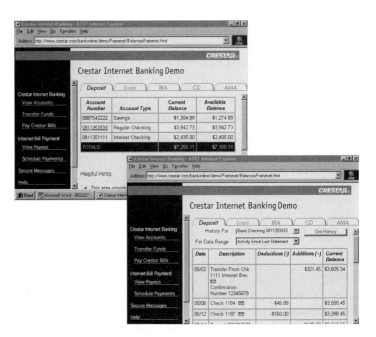

Transferring Funds

The capability of transferring funds from one account to another is simple; when you can do it online, you will feel the power in your click. The bank site will allow you to transfer funds between your accounts. It's important to know, however, whether the transfer is made in real-time. Some banks, such as CitiBank (*www.citibank.com*), for example, will let you move money from your checking account to your savings account, and the bank's system will record that transaction instantly. Other banks will let you see that you have moved the funds, but the transaction won't be official until later that day or into the next morning.

Paying Bills

If you thought transferring funds made you feel powerful, wait until you pay your bills online. Some banks offer this service for free, and others will charge you for this feature. Charges vary from bank to bank, but many offer this service free of charge for unlimited bill payment. It's good to know, too, that banks will electronically transfer the funds to some of your billers and simply cut a check to others. They will also allow you to program your site to pay certain bills each month automatically. You just have to check out the bank's policy regarding paying bills online when you pick your online bank.

One bank that has made bill paying online simple is Wingspan Bank (*www.wingspan.com*). If you have a Wingspan checking account, certificate of deposit, installment loan, credit card, or if you are an investment account customer, this service is free.

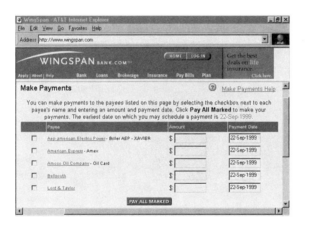

We've found that banks love to offer a bill-paying service, and have made it pretty simple. As you can see with this demonstration page from Wingspan Bank at www.wingspan.com, bill paying is simple and can save you postage.

Personalization or Customization

A lot of banks will personalize or customize a Web page for you as part of their strategy to keep you coming to their site. For example, when you first sign on to Key Bank (*www.key.com*), you are asked a series of questions. After you become a customer and you log on to the site again, the bank uses the information you provided to market other products specifically to you based on your profile. What's good about this questionnaire is that the bank even tells you why it needs certain information.

There are many different ways a bank will personalize a page for you; here is how Key Bank accomplishes that mission.

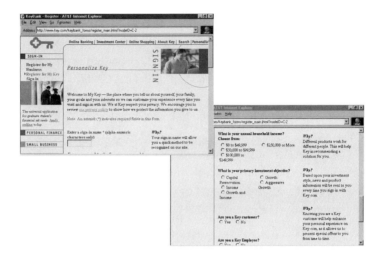

Marketplaces and Shopping Galore

Most of us aren't used to our banks selling us non-financial products. But online banks are making it easy for you to buy everything from flowers to books. Key Bank offers its customers hot links to a host of merchants. Although these links may not interest you, banks hope you will view them as your connection to e-commerce. Some banks will also offer you discounts for using affiliated merchants.

Check out this shopping center that's offered by Key Bank.

Interest-Paying Checking Accounts

Interest-paying checking accounts are a hot item for many of the pure-play Internet banks. A *pure-play Internet bank* operates in the virtual world and has no brick-and-mortar branches. The rates for these accounts vary from bank to bank, so shop around. Other checking account functions you may find offered by online banks include a calculator to reconcile your account, the ability to view canceled checks, and a way to order new checks. Who needs a teller anymore?

ATM Rebates

Offering rebates for ATM fees is fast becoming a popular item with Internet bank sites. Because some of the pure-players don't have their own ATM machines, they will offer you a rebate for charges you incur at ATMs run by other banks. This is definitely a money-saver for the customer.

> **Beware:**
> Some banks are placing limits on how many ATM refunds they will offer. Some will only offer five each month. Read the fine print in Terms and Conditions at the site or check out the frequently asked question section to see how many rebates your bank will pay.

Options to Purchase Certificates of Deposit

There's a lot of competition between banks vying for your certificates of deposit investments. Some banks will even offer better CD rates to their online customers than to those who walk into their branch offices.

On the night (yes, we like to do our online banking after-hours) we checked out a few rates, we found the following:

The national average for a three-month certificate was 4.31 percent interest rate. Wingspan was offering a three-month certificate for 5.20 percent. Not bad. But Wingspan was facing stiffer competition on other certificates. For example, Wingspan's 12-month rate was 5.85 percent to Telebank's 6.46 percent. CompuBank came in last in this three-way heat with a 5.25 percent rate for 12 months. It's definitely wise to shop around.

Mortgage Applications

After you fill out a mortgage application, some bank sites will tell you in less than a minute whether your loan is approved. You can get a new mortgage or refinance your current one at most of the sites that offer loans. Some banks will allow you to shop around and compare rates from mortgage lenders around the country.

Bank of America (*www.bankofamerica.com*) has an extensive amount of mortgage information online. When you are at the first page of the site, click Personal Finance until you can highlight and click Mortgage. From that page, you can click Mortgage again to go to extensive information about buying or refinancing a home. You can also begin filling out an application for a loan. You cannot complete the process online, but after you submit this initial information, a representative from the bank will call you to discuss your mortgage options.

One of the best reasons to at least start finding a home loan online is the amount of educational materials these bank sites give you about the process. Washington Mutual Savings Bank (*www.wamu.com*), is a good example of just how helpful these online bank mortgage sites can be. At *www.wamumortgage.com*, you can learn about your loan choices, use an online calculator to see how much you can afford, and you can learn whether you should refinance. The site even offers a step-by-step explanation about how to buy a home.

Credit Card Applications

This is definitely a product you should price around. The interest rates you'll find on cards offered online are usually the same or close to what you can get from those credit card applications mailed to you.

But as you surf from site to site looking at the different rates, you will learn that not all credit card deals are alike. On the evening we were surfing, Wachovia (*www.wachovia.com*) was offering a card at 8.25 percent with an $88 fee. First Internet Bank of Indiana (*www.firstib.com*) was offering a standard card at 12 percent with no fee. It's important to remember that there is more to a "good deal" than just the interest rate. Watch out for those fees!

The Internet is a convenient way to obtain a new card and to shop around for rates. You should also be able to review your credit card balances and recent purchases at the site from which you obtain the card.

Financial Planning Services

As the financial world gets ever more complicated and all your neighbors become wealthy day traders, financial planning services, offered by some online banks, can help you get a grip on your money matters.

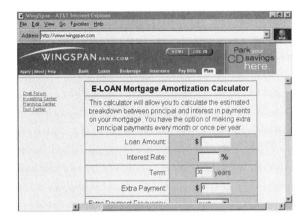

Wingspan Bank offers calculators for almost any financial transaction you want to make. Not all banks offer these features at their sites.

Each bank offers a different amount of financial advice online, but Wingspan Bank (*www.wingspan.com*) goes a step further with comprehensive financial planning. This bank's site offers you a lot of information about the financial tools available and provides several calculators so that you can see which investment is best for you. You can use an automatic loan calculator to determine how much your monthly payments will be based on your down payment, interest rate, and other factors.

Insurance Sales Options

Some sites will allow you to shop around for the best deals on all types of insurance. This sure beats word-of-mouth research.

Telebank (*www.telebank.com*) has a complete Insurance Center. At this site, you get quotes from more than 60 insurance companies. You can compare rates for auto, home, life, annuities, and other special coverage needs. There's also a 24/7 hotline available so you can discuss the options with an expert.

More and more banks will be offering insurance products as convergence of financial services continues. You'll learn more about banks and their online insurance options later in this book.

Brokerage Services

If you haven't ever purchased stock online, a bank site may be a good place to go to start. Some Internet banks offer research tools and a place to actually buy and sell your stocks.

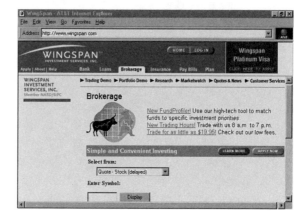

Each stock transaction at Wingspan Bank costs $19.95, but the online bank certainly makes these transactions easy.

Ability to Interface with Your Existing Software

Some online banks can recognize and interface with the money management tools or software on your computer. If you already have this kind of software to manage your money, some bank sites will interact with Intuit's Quicken or Microsoft's Money. For example, you can download account information to balance your checkbook, manage your personal budget, and do long-range financial planning.

Twenty-Four-Hour Telephone Access to a Real Banker

As we surfed banking sites and as we do our own online banking, we have found that access to a 24-hour honest-to-goodness *real* banker to be an invaluable service. Although this service may cost the bank more money, good customer service will definitely attract and keep customers. Fees and costs are important, but this service allows one online bank a great advantage over another. If your bank doesn't have its customer service number prominently displayed, call or email the bank and tell it that it should.

Internet Access

A few banks are Internet service providers that can offer their customers access to the World Wide Web. Some do this so that they can offer discounted prices to their customers or because they are located in a rural area where there isn't a local number to dial up a national ISP.

Bay-Vanguard Federal Savings Bank, located in Baltimore, Maryland (*www.bayvanguard.com*), serves as an Internet Service Provider to its customers. This bank took this extra step to help its customers afford getting online.

Your bank wants you to go online for financial services; as a result, providing Internet access is a natural fit for a bank. However, the latest twist is for a bank to partner with ISPs as a way to provide their customers access to the World Wide Web.

Helpful Information for Tax Purposes

Some banks will show you the interest you have earned on certain accounts to help make preparing your taxes more convenient and accurate. CompuBank is an all-around winner in the services it offers, including interest information for tax purposes. You can learn about the interest you've earned from all banks in monthly statements, but CompuBank doesn't make you hunt around for the information, and it will provide that data on a daily basis.

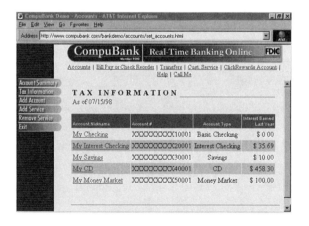

Here is a personalized page that CompuBank will provide for you showing the interest you have earned on your accounts.

Privacy and Security

Guarantees of privacy and security aren't really a product or a service. They should represent a basic reality of any online banking site. We explain all the privacy and security matters that you need to know about in Part III, "The Facts About Security and Privacy," of this book. We briefly mention them here because these matters should always be at the top of your concerns.

A Few Words of Caution: There Are Some Risks

We are big fans of online banking, but we would be remiss if we didn't share a few insider concerns about Internet banking. Don't let these observations stop you from banking online, but use them to be a smarter consumer.

Although banks are taking steps every day to make their sites safe and secure from hackers, e-thieves are at work also, always inventing ways to crack systems thought to be secure. So there is some risk in banking online. The Office of the Comptroller of the Currency, which is the regulator of national banks, notes the following risks:

- Informational-only sites could have their advertising messages altered by hackers.

- Electronic mail containing confidential information could be sent in error to the wrong recipient.

- Some banks have their systems connected to other businesses, a setup that can offer an opportunity to thieves who want to access sensitive information.

The Comptroller also lists natural disasters as a possible risk to your bank's system. Because the Internet spans the world, an interruption caused by a natural disaster such as an earthquake or tornado could bring the system down.

One concern banks have isn't solely focused on online banking; it also includes their brick-and-mortar operations. This concern is illegal access to their customers' files by dishonest employees. The risk of a system broach is not always from outside the bank, sometimes it comes from the inside.

The U.S. General Accounting Office, which investigates a host of government matters, released a report last year saying that Internet banking world was not all up to speed. The GAO conducted an investigation to evaluate the effectiveness of the bank regulators' examinations of Internet banking operations. "First, we found that Internet banking heightens various types of traditional banking risks and our review of 81 examinations showed that roughly 44 percent of the depository institutions examined had not completely implemented risk-management steps that regulators said are needed to limit online banking risks," the GAO stated. Some of the shortcomings noted a lack of approval of a strategic plan by boards of directors and a lack of policies and procedures for Internet banking operations. The GAO added to its report that its observations couldn't be extended throughout the industry because not enough bank examinations had been conducted as of May 1999. One reason for this was because bank regulators were having to spend an extra amount of time handling century date change matters.

Take heed of these concerns from the government, but don't let them stop you from entering the new age in banking anywhere, anytime.

What You Should Know Now

After reading through this chapter, you should now possess the following information:

- There are information-only and transactional online bank sites. Because you have a choice, you want the transactional site so that you can take control of your accounts.

- Click the demonstration or "demo" links at different banking sites to learn which one fits you best.

- Shop around. Banks are offering a long list of services, including traditional financial services and shopping.

- There's no need to worry that your information isn't safe on the Internet. However, you should keep informed of the goings-on in e-banking and know that nothing is risk-free in *real* life or on the World Wide Web.

CHAPTER 3
What You'll Need for Online Banking

In Chapter 2, "What Online Banking Means for You," we discussed the online banking trend and what it means for you as a tool for more active financial management. Now let's get down to business by looking at what tools you need to do your banking online.

You're thinking you've got a personal computer and a pipeline to the information highway in the form of an Internet service provider. What else do you need? Surprisingly, not much. But there are several things that you should consider as you begin your online banking experience, including whether you will want to consolidate all your personal finances under one roof (a growing trend) or use a personal financial management software product, also known as a *financial suite*.

What You'll Learn in This Chapter:
- In the beginning, there was direct dial.
- The three types of online banking.
- How your computer connects to the bank.
- What a financial suite is and how it works with your bank's system.

A History Lesson: Proprietary Evolves into Open Systems

Just a few years ago, Microsoft Chairman Bill Gates proclaimed that "banks are dinosaurs," a comment that sent shudders through oak-paneled bank boardrooms from Manhattan to San Francisco. However, comments like his and the slow recognition of the popularity of personal financial management software encouraged banks to become bolder in developing and providing online banking services. We'll leave the dinosaur debate to the futurists, but we feel safe in saying that virtually every bank in the country is at least considering online banking as a way of better serving and retaining their customers (that's you).

Fun Fact:
The first Internet-only bank, Security First Network Bank at *www.sfnb.com*, received its charter (permission to operate as a legitimate bank) in 1995.

The Way It Used to Be

Online banking, in its initial phase less than a decade ago, was once the province of mostly larger banks that could afford to make huge technology investments in "proprietary" systems. Banks offering online services typically developed their own software, which they distributed to their customers. The software enabled customers to communicate directly with their banks by using their personal computers and a modem connection.

Although these early initiatives were a good start to what we're seeing today in online financial services, they were not without flaws. Aside from limited functionality, the early proprietary online systems were hindered by a severe lack of demand. The number of household PCs was relatively small, a fact that gave banks limited justification to continue refining and improving their proprietary online offerings.

> **Grandma Wouldn't Recognize Today's Online Banking**
>
> In its earliest form, personal computer-based home banking meant using proprietary software from your bank. Your institution would send you a disk containing this software, which you then had to load onto your computer.
>
> The proprietary software would enable you to dial up your bank's computer system using a modem; after you were connected, you could conduct limited banking functions.
>
> As you may be guessing, this system never became very popular. The proprietary software didn't always run properly because there was a big lack of standardization among PCs, software, and communications protocols. Also, because the bank's software was *proprietary*—only for use in connecting and communicating with a particular bank—customers were limited in their options.
>
> Yet another problem with widespread use of proprietary home banking software was that—believe it or not—some banks charged for the service.
>
> Today, the Internet, faster, more standardized computer products and software, and quicker modems have broken down these earlier online banking hurdles. If you've got a newer PC, a modem, and an Internet service provider, you can be banking online on short notice. Plus, you're not locked into any particular bank's proprietary software system.

The New Way to Bank

The development and acceptance of household PCs and the Internet has changed the earlier paradigm. With the connectivity capabilities of the Internet, banks have worked with a variety of third-party software providers. They have also worked together in cooperative ventures to develop the necessary interfaces to seamlessly bridge the distance between your home computer and your bank's information-processing system.

Banks are increasingly emphasizing having "open," browser-based online banking systems instead of "proprietary" setups. This means portability for you because you're not locked into a particular bank's exclusive software. It also means ease of use. If you can use a Web browser, such as Internet Explorer or Netscape Navigator, you can bank online (well, at least you can after you finish reading this book).

At this point, you might be asking yourself why some banks invested money in online banking systems that never got off the ground. When they did so, the Internet was a nascent concept, so the only option available for banks to ensure security and provide connectivity for their online customers was the development of proprietary software and interfaces to accounting information. Although they were a little clumsy and basic, these early offerings provided a learning experience for banks that has helped build a foundation for the online financial services environment of today—and tomorrow. Citibank, however, one of the major electronic banking leaders, continues to provide both direct-dial and true Internet banking.

Direct-dial banking means that you use your computer and modem to dial up your bank's computer to transact business. In such a system, an Internet connection is not necessary. The only requirement is a modem and a telephone line. *Internet banking*, which we're referring to in this book as *online banking*, relies on connecting to the Internet through your computer's modem and Web browser software.

The Three Ways of Banking Online

Today, online banking generally takes place in one of three ways:

> **Netscape This, Netscape That:**
> Netscape Communicator is a package of Web software products that includes Netscape Navigator, the popular Web browser software. In effect, Navigator is a part of Netscape Communicator's landscape.

- *Over the Internet*—Using secure Web browser software such as Netscape Navigator or Internet Explorer. These browsers enable consumers to access their account information through their online bank's Web site. This route to banking online requires the use of Internet browsers that support 128-bit encryption, such as Netscape Communicator 4.06, Netscape Navigator 4.06, or Microsoft Internet Explorer (version 4.0 or later). Your Internet service provider or online bank can help you obtain the correct version of these browser products. At many of these bank sites, you can actually download browser software onto your hardware. The 128-bit level of encryption of the latest Web browsers protects consumers by scrambling all the personal information transmitted between a customer's home computer and the bank.

- *Using personal financial management software products (such as Quicken or Money)*—These products have the capability to exchange information with your online bank, if your bank supports such a connection. This approach represents a combination of browser-based online banking with personal financial management software that customers are operating on their home computers.

- *Using proprietary software from your online bank*—This is software provided by your bank that operates on your computer. The software typically enables consumers to connect to the bank over a telephone line. The features and functions may range from basic transactions to more sophisticated services, such as tracking investments. Some people in the e-commerce world don't consider this truly online banking because you dial directly into the bank's computer and your data doesn't flow through the Internet. This proprietary approach to remote banking is also called *PC banking*.

WHAT YOU'LL NEED FOR ONLINE BANKING

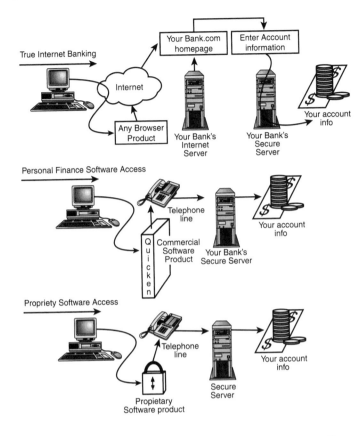

There are three ways to bank online. As you can see, all three must access your account information through your bank's secure server.

▼ **Try It Yourself**

1. Connect to the Internet and fire up your Web browser. Go to the Bank of America home page at *www.bankofamerica.com*. Click Learn More to learn more about online banking.

2. Click Online Banking under Personal Options. At the next screen, select your state. Then click Demo to start the Bank of America's online banking demonstration.

   Congratulations! You have ventured out on your own to learn firsthand about online banking.

3. Now try something else: Return to the first screen in step 2 (the one that lists Personal Options). This time, instead of clicking Online Banking, click PC Banking with Managing Your Money. Read the information here and then click the

Demo button. You'll learn about how online banking works with the Microsoft Money personal financial management software. Note that Bank of America's Money-compatible online banking system relies on a direct-line dial-up connection between your PC and the bank.

Strike Up the Bandwidth

What does it take to get connected to an online bank? You need a home computer, of course, equipped with Web browser software such as Internet Explorer or Netscape Navigator.

You're also going to need an Internet service provider (ISP) to serve as your computer's gateway to the World Wide Web. Another important component is how you connect to your ISP, such as through a telephone modem (we recommend as fast a connection as you can get—a minimum of 56K) or a cable modem.

Connecting with a Telephone Modem

A *telephone modem* adapts a terminal or computer to a telephone line. It converts the computer's digital pulses into audio frequencies (analog). At the other end, the receiving modem converts the analog frequencies back into digital pulses. The modem also dials the line, answers the call, and controls transmission speed. Although modems have come in speeds of 300; 1,200; 2,400; 9,600; 14,400; 28,800 (28.8Kbps); 33,300 (33.3Kbps); and 56,000 (56Kbps) bits per second, today higher speeds are typically used in the latter only.

The software required to use a modem depends on what kind of service you want. A connection to an ISP requires a Web browser and TCP/IP networking protocols, both of which are either provided by the ISP or are included with the operating system, such as Windows 95/98 and NT. The online services (such as America Online, CompuServe, and so on) generally provide the required software and dial-up utilities.

All new modems have built-in error correction and data compression. For files that are already compressed, the hardware data compression adds little value because it cannot make compressed

Bits and Baud:
The term *baud* is a techie term that comes from the days of the Eniac computer. It is used to mean exactly the same thing as *bits per second*. When you talk about a 56KB baud modem, and your friend talks about a 56Kbps modem, you're both talking about the same thing.

files smaller. Modems also have automatic feature negotiation, which adjusts to the speed and hardware protocols of the modem on the other end of the line.

Connecting with a Cable Modem

A *cable modem* is used to connect a computer to a cable television service that provides Internet access. Cable modems can dramatically increase the bandwidth between a person's home computer and their ISP. Cable modems link to the computer with Ethernet, which provides online service all the time. However, Ethernet is a shared medium, and the connection speed varies depending on how many customers on that cable segment are using the Web at the same time.

There are specific requirements for hooking up to the Internet with a cable modem. You'll want to check with your local cable access provider, but the following are some basic considerations:

- Depending on how your neighborhood is wired for cable, a connection can be either one-way or two-way.

- A *one-way connection* means that you access the Internet using your computer's telephone modem. The benefit of the higher-speed cable modem enters the picture when you download Web pages to your PC.

- A *two-way connection* uses the cable modem for both upstream (your computer to the Internet) and downstream (the Internet to your PC) communications.

- The higher-speed benefits can be obtained in both the one-way and two-way systems because, for most Internet users, the majority of communications go from the Internet to the PC.

Generally, your cable company will provide you with a list of specifications. Some companies will install the necessary Ethernet card and ensure that everything is optimal for your Internet connection. The cost of cable modem access runs from $40 and up per month.

> **Fun Fact:**
> Cable television was invented on Thanksgiving Day in 1948 by Ed Parsons. He gathered his family around the television set in Astoria, Oregon, to watch a broadcast from a UHF station based in Seattle using an antenna amplifier he had designed. Ed Parsons thus became the first Cable Guy.

If you're currently using a dedicated telephone line for your Internet access, a cable modem set-up is in a similar price range. A good site for more information about cable modem is *www.cablemodemhelp.com*.

We can't say enough about the speed of your connection to the Internet. With online banking, you're receiving and sending a lot of information through the pipeline (security measures also add to the amount of bits and bytes flowing). Thus, the bigger your pipeline is, the faster and more productive your online banking experience will become.

What *Is* Bandwidth, Anyway?

Bandwidth is the expression used to describe the transmission capacity of an electronic line, such as a communications network. The greater the bandwidth of a communications line, the higher the carrying capacity that line has. Bandwidth is expressed in *bits per second*, *bytes per second*, or in *Hertz* (cycles per second). When expressed in Hertz, the frequency may be a greater number than the actual bits per second because the bandwidth is the difference between the lowest and highest frequencies transmitted.

Bear in mind that bandwidth is an issue being addressed by virtually all the players involved in computer technology, the Internet, and e-commerce. In this regard, we expect online banking systems to become faster and better in the future. In the meantime, we suggest that you take steps now to make your connections to the Internet and online banking as smooth and as fast as possible.

What's the Function of Financial Suites?

The folks at Intuit Inc. (who developed the popular personal financial management software product Quicken) and Microsoft (which developed Microsoft Money, another leading personal financial management software program) have helped push the online banking envelope. Why? With the growing popularity of personal financial management software, these two companies could foresee the integration of their software with online banking several years ago. This was before more than a handful of banks were offering online banking.

Intuit and Microsoft both have Web sites designed to highlight their personal financial management software products and to serve as "portals" to the world of online financial services, similar to how Yahoo! and AOL are portals to the broader world of the Internet. Intuit and Microsoft have worked hard to ensure that their software is compatible with most online banking systems, so that information from an online bank—your statement balance and cleared checks, for example—can be downloaded into your personal financial management software.

Bank Where You Surf:

In this world where everyone is trying to offer you everything on the Web, it's interesting to note that both Yahoo! and AOL feature "banking centers" at their sites.

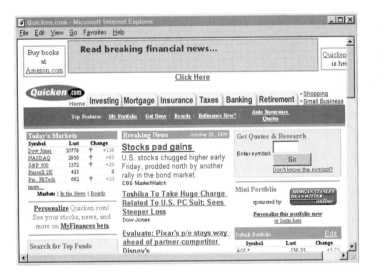

The Quicken home page (www.quicken.com) provides access to all the financial information you need when you're using the Intuit Quicken personal financial software.

Both Intuit's Quicken Web site and Microsoft's Money Web site provide the look and feel of financial portals, providing an array of news and information, as well as links to their personal financial management software suites and to online banks.

The Microsoft MoneyCentral home page (http://moneycentral.msn.com/home) provides links to many areas of financial interest. If you use Microsoft Money, you'll visit this site often.

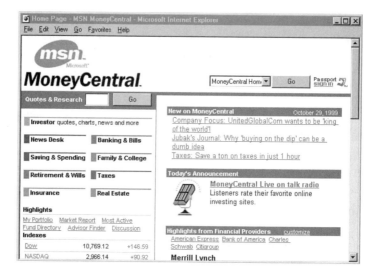

If you're a devoted user of Quicken or Money—and there are many—you'll want to make sure that your online bank's system will operate in a manner that complements how you currently use your personal financial management software.

More powerful versions of Quicken and Money software products enable users to track their investments, manage their bank accounts, and manage the books of their businesses. If you're planning to conduct online banking through one provider while managing your investments with another, either of these personal financial management software products can help you control and manage all your financial activities.

In the meantime, both Intuit and Microsoft have sought partnerships with banks to promote both their software products and online banking. Banks have developed strategic partnerships with major Internet portals such as America Online and Yahoo!—as have specialty financial services companies, such as Countrywide Mortgage (a national mortgage lender) and discount brokerage firms, such as Charles Schwab and e*Trade. If all this smacks of convergence, you're partly right, but it's also indicative of new markets and new services being explored, developed, and tested.

For banks and other financial services providers, the opportunities and explorations into the world of the Internet and e-commerce are part of ongoing research and development that will ultimately benefit both the successful providers and their customers.

All these new initiatives, joint ventures, and strategic partnerships can be confusing. A competitive, relatively low-cost service arena like the Internet is an utterly confusing marketplace at times. Our advice when it comes to online banking: Survey your options, learn what's new, and stay up to date. There is a constant stream of innovation occurring, which is good for you as a consumer (and good for us, as book authors).

What You Should Know Now

In this chapter, we've examined some of the history of home-based PC banking, which shows how far and how fast technology, the Internet, and financial services providers have come in building an entirely new delivery channel for you to use to manage your finances.

Let's recap:

- In the beginning, there was a direct-dial connection between a bank and a customer, typically through proprietary software that came from the bank. This has changed for the better. The Internet and computer hardware and software standardization now make it possible to quickly and easily connect with an online bank.

- There are three types of online banking: through the Internet; through personal financial management software products, such as Quicken and Money; and by dialing up your bank directly using software provided by the bank. The latter approach is becoming much less common as the Internet continues to expand.

- With Internet banking—which we call *online banking*—your computer connects to your bank through Web browser software, such as Internet Explorer or Netscape Navigator. You'll want to make sure that you're using the latest versions of either of those products to ensure that you get the full benefits of all the security that comes built into those products (we'll discuss these security features in detail later).

- The Quicken and Money financial suites are popular financial management software tools that are often supported by online banking services providers. If you're a user of either of these products, you'll want to consider how you'll continue to use them after you've connected to your online bank.

CHAPTER 4

Choosing Your Bank

Shopping for an online bank may seem simple, but it can be a bit daunting and bewildering. For one thing, there's no lack of information on the topic when you log on to the Internet.

Meanwhile, back in the dirt world (or back to our offline existence), you're probably hearing about online banking on television and radio and reading advertisements about Internet banking in newspapers and magazines. The competition is fierce for your business, and banks are spending big bucks to get you to bank with them in the cyber world.

First Internet Bank of Indiana, at *www.firstib.com*, spent $800,000 in just one four-month period to get your money into their e-accounts. One of this institution's slogans is "Bank Naked. Do your banking at Firstib.com no matter what you are wearing. Or not wearing." This bank is even advertising overseas. It's based in America's heartland, but it has customers from Florida to California to military bases around world. David Becker, president of the bank, told us that five percent of his customers live outside the country or are travelers.

You may have even received a flyer or a brochure from your current bank encouraging you to consider banking online. Remember the discussion in Chapter 2, "What Online Banking Means to You," about why banks want us to go online? Online banking can save banks money while providing consumers with faster, more convenient service. When they keep you out of their teller lines, they have fewer tellers to pay.

Selecting an online bank will require you to think about how you currently use your financial institution, whether it's a bank, credit union, or savings and loan. How often in the past month have you had reason to visit one of your bank's offices in person? If you

What You'll Learn in This Chapter:
- ▶ How to shop for online banking services.
- ▶ Online banking features you'll want and need.
- ▶ One-stop shopping Internet portals.

own a small business, you'll need to consider the banking products and services you're using in that regard, as well as how often you need to personally visit your bank to deposit checks or conduct other types of business. We'll look more closely at online banking for small businesses in Chapter 10, "Online Banking for Small Business Owners."

Shopping for Online Banking Services

Type the phrase *online banking* into any major search engine such as Yahoo!, Google, Alta Vista, Excite, Hotbot, or AskJeeves, and you'll get hundreds of references. Many of those references will relate to banks offering online services. Others will be links to companies that advise institutions how to get online or that provide the systems for them to enter the electronic world. There also will be several references to companies pointing out a few good deals.

Making sense of it all is a challenge. We're here to help.

The Big Net Approach

You have two options when you go shopping for an online bank. You can throw out a big net by searching for a broad term, such as online banking, and haul in thousands of matches, or you can try a more focused approach. Because we like to go fishing, let's first see what happens when we keep the search broad.

Try It Yourself

1. Let's try a search on Google.com (*www.google.com*). In the search box, type the phrase *online banking*. When we did this, the search engine gave us 21,358 entries plus a banner ad teasing us about interest on a checking account at six percent.

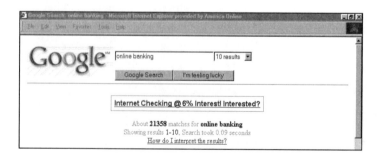

Google.com returns thousands of entries when we typed the phrase *online banking* in the search box.

2. If you're as curious as we were, click the banner ad. We found ourselves face to face with CaroLine, the online banking service of Carolina First Bank of Columbia, South Carolina.

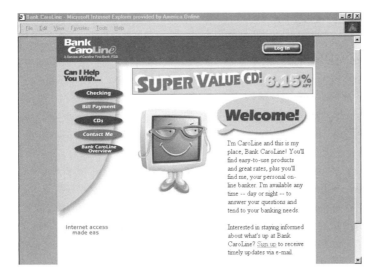

Clicking a banner ad on the Google results page took us directly to CaroLine, the online banking service of Carolina First Bank of Columbia, S.C.

3. In hot pursuit of that six percent yield on your hard-earned dollars, click the Checking button. A page opens to tell you that you can "earn up to 6 percent" annual percentage yield.

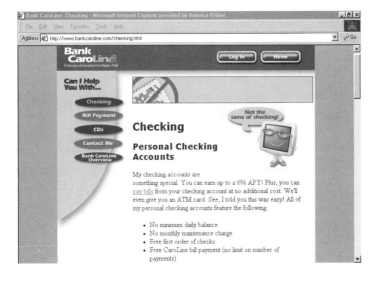

Clicking the Checking button took us to a page explaining how we could "earn up to 6 percent" annual percentage yield.

4. Don't think that the Internet is paved with gold just yet! Scroll down the page to find that to get the high interest rate, you'll have to commit a minimum of 25,000 scoots for a high-yielding CD checking account.

To get that attractive interest rate will require a balance of $25,000 or more.

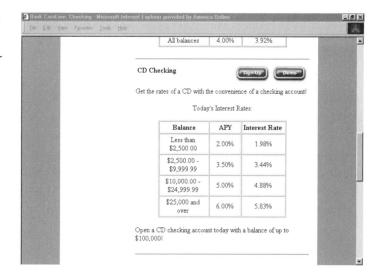

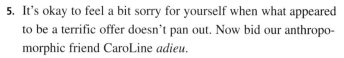

5. It's okay to feel a bit sorry for yourself when what appeared to be a terrific offer doesn't pan out. Now bid our anthropomorphic friend CaroLine *adieu*.

The Focused Search

Our brief foray into cyberspace shows how banks use teaser rates and other enticements on the Internet to get consumers to visit their online banking sites. Surprise. This differs little from the physical world in which institutions use newspapers, radio, and television to sell you their products and services.

We suggest that you take a more targeted approach in shopping for online banking services.

Start with Your Current Bank

If you like the products and services you're getting from your current bank or credit union, we suggest you give them a serious look as your online bank. By transitioning to online banking through your current institution, you may be able to save some money in fees, as well as save the time and costs associated with switching banks. (These costs can include having new checks printed and establishing new direct-deposit services for your paychecks.)

Begin with the bank or credit union that currently handles your checking account. Does it offer online banking services? If so, does the online banking system include features such as electronic bill payment? Will the bank's system support a financial management suite such as Quicken or Money?

You'll want to ask questions. Check your bank's Web site. Look for a privacy policy and read it. Look at the fee structures. Compare your current bank's Web site with others in your local market. Although it's certainly not impossible to establish a relationship with an online bank virtually anywhere in the world, it may be more convenient and comforting to know that you can always visit a local, physical branch should problems arise.

You'll also want to test drive your bank's online system. Most institutions provide online banking demos for consumers to conduct test transactions. The demos also provide a look at how an account statement appears and how it can be used to track your payments and deposits. We're going to get more detailed on how to do specific types of transactions in Chapter 7, "No Postage Necessary: Paying Bills Online," and Chapter 8, "Beyond the Basics: Cool Add-On Products and Services." For a look at what a typical online banking demo opening page looks like, let's go to the site of Bay-Vanguard Federal Savings Bank at *www.bayvanguard.com*. This bank is based in Baltimore, Maryland.

▼ **Try It Yourself**

1. Open the home page of the Bay-Vanguard Federal Savings Bank site at *www.bayvanguard.com*.

2. Under Internet Banking, click Learn More.

3. Access the online banking demo by clicking the Access Accounts button. An account summary page opens, providing details on two checking accounts, a certificate of deposit account, a home equity loan, and a car loan.

When you view the account demo at Bay-Vanguard's Web site, you can see an account summary page. For details about the transaction history for an account, click its balance.

4. Click the highlighted balance of the Household Checking account to see a detailed statement page showing deposits to the account and checks written on the account.

The Bay-Vanguard account demo provides a detailed statement page showing deposits to the account and checks written on the account. You can delve farther by clicking the various buttons or transactions on this page.

5. You can get more information about accounts and practice making transactions by clicking the various buttons on the detailed statement page.

> **No PC? No Problem!**
>
> What if you're interested in Internet banking but you haven't bought that souped-up home computer just yet? Don't worry—most financial institutions offering online banking have PCs in their branch offices for their customers to use to test the service.
>
> The workstations in the branch office provide an excellent way for you to become comfortable with cyber banking. You'll also score valuable face time, we hope, with a knowledgeable staff person. We've been both disappointed and pleased with the bankers we've visited. We don't think you should be a rough and tough customer, but you should be a smart one: Insist on talking to someone who knows the bank's online operation thoroughly.
>
> Remember, banks want you to go online. This saves them time and money while providing you with new convenience and capabilities.
>
> You'll want to ask questions of the bank's staff during your demo. Ask about security, privacy, the speed of the demo PC's Internet connection, and how your institution can get you up and running. Ask about fees, too, as well as all the features and functions available.
>
> If your bank offers the in-house demo, use it. It's an excellent way to gauge first-hand a bank's commitment to online banking.

Shop Nationwide for an Online Bank

If your current bank or credit union doesn't offer online banking, you'll need to shop around some more. Again, we encourage you to first look locally and see what's being offered and the fees involved.

Start surfing. You may even notice that some online banking sites look similar in terms of how account information is accessed and displayed. This happens because several institutions are using the same online banking software. This software becomes the basic architecture of their sites—just as mass-produced homes can all look alike, so do many banking sites.

Still looking for the right online banking fit? Let's go shopping nationwide.

1. For a list of online banks and credit unions, try bankonline.com at *www.bankonline.com*. This site presents a list of online banking providers around the world, sorted by geographic region, country and state, or other governmental jurisdiction.

▼ **Try It Yourself**

2. Individual listings in the directory are hot links. Click a listed bank or credit union's name to go to that particular provider's online banking Web site.

   This directory, by the way, is growing each day. BankoOnline.com encourages feedback from consumers about new online banking sites.

3. Scroll through the list of banks to get an idea of just how widespread this online banking movement is. Although we're not planning to move to New Zealand just yet, we're happy to know that we can locate a list of online banking providers there should the need arise.

Online Banking Features You May Want and Need

Basic online banking features include having the ability to view your checking and savings accounts over the Internet and to perform transactions such as moving money from your savings account to checking account and vice versa. Let's look at some additional features you might want to consider.

Following Your Money

Most browser-based online banking systems allow you to view your accounts and recent transactions. This is a handy money management tool and it beats going to a branch or an ATM to have a statement of recent account activity printed out. By simply going online, you can look at your checking account and find out if your Aunt Essie cashed that birthday check you sent her or if your payment to your local utility company has cleared.

Typically, when viewing a checking account or *money market account* (a type of account that allows you a limited number of check payments each month), you'll have two options. You can view the *account statement*, which is your online bank's official reckoning of your account and recent activity, or you can view your *account register*, which is similar to the paper record of deposits and checks that you keep with your checkbook. It's not unusual when comparing your online bank's statement and your register to find differences. Some payments or deposits listed in your register may not have been cleared by your bank and, as a result, may not be listed in your statement.

Paying Bills Online

Online bill payment allows you to pay bills over the Internet. We'll explore paying bills online in greater detail in Chapter 7. Basically, through online bill payment, you are authorizing your bank to pay someone a certain amount of money.

It's very much like writing and mailing a check for your mortgage or rent every month. However, instead of putting the check in an envelope and paying for the postage to send it, your online bank does it. Sometimes, if the company you are paying is big, the bank sends your online bill payment electronically. In other cases, your bank creates a physical check that it mails for you.

Some online banks charge a fee for this service, typically a set amount per month for a given number of payments, such as $5.95 for 20 online bill payments. Others do not charge a fee for online bill payment. This can be an important consideration. In most cases, however, the monthly fee is typically lower than the equivalent postage for the maximum number of items each month ($5.95 divided by 20 payments is roughly 30 cents, less than 20 33-cent stamps—not counting the cost of the checks).

Most banks that charge for online bill payment allow customers to opt out and still enjoy other benefits of online banking.

Applying for Loans

Applying for a loan can certainly be faster and easier online. Loan products, such as credit cards, overdraft lines of credit (used only when and if you should overdraw a checking account), auto loans, personal loans, educational loans, and even home equity and mortgage loans can be applied for online. Still, you'll want to shop around and compare rates first.

Most online bank sites have loan calculators that can help you determine how much your monthly payment would be under different loan terms (such as the length of time for repayment), interest rates, and loan balances). This is a very helpful feature that can you help you shop better for any type of a loan product.

Other Features to Look For

Other features to look for in online banking include the ability to open new accounts. Still more: How about tracking your mutual fund or stock and bond investments along with your checking and savings accounts and loans?

Although such all-in-one online banking sites are the exception today rather than the rule, we expect online banks to enhance their services to become more like one-stop personal financial management providers.

Portals to Banking and Finance

In some respects, Internet portals such as America Online (AOL), the Microsoft Network (MSN), and Yahoo! resemble all-in-one shops for financial services. AOL's banking center, for example, features business news and investment information, as well as providing help with shopping for a mortgage loan, insurance, and online banking services.

Are the financial pages of portals such as AOL and Yahoo! banks? No. As they're currently constructed, think of them as a very busy bazaar that you're trying to shop quickly. As you make your way through the links attempting to find what you're looking for, you're forced to hear (actually, read) boisterous pitches from all the bazaar's many merchants.

At the MSN portal, you can't miss the ads for NetBank.com. This Internet-only bank cut a deal with MSN last year that will ensure that its banners will be displayed prominently throughout the portal. NetBank is hoping to attract some of MSN's five million visitors each month to its own products and services.

The portals do provide avenues to locating financial services providers, including online banking sites. Bear in mind, however, that the portals aren't exactly disinterested third parties merely providing links and information. Banks and other financial services providers pay the portals to be listed on their sites, typically at a rate that increases with prominence.

CHOOSING YOUR BANK

AOL's banking center features news and information as well as shopping help in finding financial products and services. Buyer beware, however. These banks have paid AOL a fee to be listed here. Note that Quicken.com is credited for creating this portion of AOL's portal.

Yahoo's banking page features a pitch for Telebank, which is becoming primarily an online bank, as well as links to bank and banking-related providers and information.

A Community Bank as an ISP

One of the more interesting facets of the banking industry's transition to online banking is the role of the Internet. Without it, there would be no customers to serve in the online world.

With that said, people also need a way to get on to the Internet. This is the role played by an Internet service provider, or ISP. AOL and MindSpring, for example, are ISPs.

continues

continued

> Faced with an aging customer base, Bay-Vanguard Federal Savings Bank, a small one-office Baltimore-based community bank, thought outside of the box two years ago as its senior staff pondered the possibilities of online banking.
>
> Although the bank was committed to providing Internet banking services—which appeals to younger customers—it faced a potentially gigantic hurdle because of limited access among its customers to the Internet. The bank surmised that traditional ISPs were too expensive for its customers. Bay-Vanguard's solution? Establish its own ISP.
>
> Novel, yes. So novel that the institution's primary regulator—the Office of Thrift Supervision—had rarely if ever encountered such an application for a new activity before. We're happy to note that two years later, Bay-Vanguard's ISP is doing well, as is its online banking site.

What You Should Know Now

This chapter covered the basics of shopping for online banking services, as well as some of the features you'll need as the chief executive officer of You, Inc. The following is a summary of what you should have learned:

- Shop locally. Ask what your current bank can do for you online.

- Take advantage of in-person online banking demos at a local bank or credit union and test demo features of online banking systems on the Internet.

- Think about the features you'll need and use in online banking and compare those features and fees from several online banks.

CHAPTER 5

Ready, Set, Stop: Do Your Due Diligence

Let's say that you've found the perfect online bank. You followed our shopping tips in Chapter 4, "Choosing Your Bank," test drove several demos, and feel comfortable about beginning your online banking experience for real in the virtual realm of cyberspace.

This chapter is about taking a breather and doing some due diligence on your online bank. While we're not going to hit you on the head and say "Stop what you're doing," we would like to give you some valuable tips about checking up on your online bank before getting down to business. (These tips will work for real world banks, too. Trust us.)

Why? Because of the tremendous growth of the Internet over the past decade, there have been a variety of online scams reported. Among these have been con artists purporting to be online banks or purporting to sell legitimate investment products.

Cons like these and others are designed to separate unwary people from their money. Aside from the economic damage they do to consumers, they also undermine confidence in online banking and finance, and e-commerce in general.

It pays to be wary (you'll sleep better, for one thing). Most Internet and e-commerce participants, including online banks, are wary, too. They want consumers to feel safe and secure about transacting business online.

Banking regulators want consumers to feel safe and secure, too. That's why they periodically examine banks and credit unions to make sure that nothing is amiss. Regulators also require quarterly reports on the financial condition of an institution.

What You'll Learn in This Chapter:
- The importance of the FDIC label.
- How deposit insurance works.
- The consumer protection regulations.

An upside to the Internet: The bank and credit union regulatory agencies all have Web sites that provide a wealth of consumer information, financial calculators, shopping tips, and other features. This is very much an example of the government working for and on behalf of American consumers.

Look for the FDIC Label

For consumers, one of the most important aspects of bank and credit union regulation is deposit insurance. The Federal Deposit Insurance Corporation (FDIC) insures consumers' deposit accounts up to $100,000. For credit unions, deposits—commonly referred to as *shares* because depositors are member/owners of their respective credit unions—are insured for the same amount by the National Credit Union Administration.

In the event of a federally insured bank or credit union failure, depositors are protected up to $100,000, with some partial leeway for accrued interest. In other words, *accrued interest* (money you're owed) through the date of a financial institution's closing or failure, is included when calculating insurance coverage. It's also important to note that deposit insurance can be expanded, depending on how you structure your accounts among individual accounts and joint accounts.

This is a complex issue, but one you might want to familiarize yourself with if your checking and savings accounts, including certificates of deposit, would or could exceed $100,000. Even though it may be unlikely now, your deposits could possibly exceed $100,000 in the future if you should sell your house or an investment property or receive a lump-sum retirement distribution or life insurance settlement.

The FDIC has a feature at its Web site called EDIE, which can help you calculate where you and your family stand regarding deposit insurance. EDIE stands for the Electronic Deposit Insurance Estimator. Through an interview format, the system takes you through all types of possible account relationships and nuances.

Understanding how deposit insurance coverage can work can be a challenge. Even bank staff members sometimes have difficulty

Fun Fact:

Congress created the Federal Deposit Insurance Corporation in 1933 to restore public confidence in the nation's banking system. President Franklin D. Roosevelt viewed this as a mistake because it created a "moral hazard" for banks. Roosevelt thought deposit insurance created an incentive for banks to take on excessive risk.

explaining it to consumers. The FDIC's estimator goes a very long way in helping consumers calculate their deposit insurance coverage. (What's this—a bank regulatory agency getting friendly?) The FDIC's home page at *www.fdic.gov* is shown in the following figure.

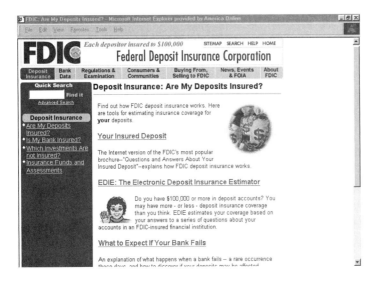

Note EDIE, the Electronic Deposit Insurance Estimator, smiling and waving. She's there to help you sort out your deposit insurance coverage.

Why Worry About Deposit Insurance?

When a bank fails, the regulatory agencies involved (see our accompanying discussion) usually try to arrange for a resolution called a *purchase and assumption*. In such a transaction, a healthy bank assumes most of the deposits and loans of the failed bank.

As part of the transaction, the FDIC, as the insurer of deposits, assumes the remaining portion of deposits and loans. Although it sounds complex, this is meant to encourage a healthy bank to purchase the majority of a failed bank's assets (loans) and liabilities (deposits).

When the FDIC becomes the receiver (the manager) of a failed bank, depositors of more than $100,000 may face the prospect of a "haircut," meaning that they may not receive the full value of their deposits in excess of the $100,000 coverage level.

> **Fun Fact:**
> The oldest federal bank regulatory agency is probably the least well known. The Office of the Comptroller of the Currency was established in 1863 as part of legislation creating a system of national banks to issue national currency that would help finance the Civil War.

Case in point: Consider the closure in September 1999 of First National Bank of Keystone, West Virginia, by the Office of the Comptroller of the Currency, which regulates national banks. According to the FDIC, the failed bank had local uninsured deposits totaling approximately $15 million in 500 accounts (an average of $30,000 per account).

These account holders with uninsured funds (in excess of the $100,000 limit) join other creditors (parties owed money) of the failed institution and have no guarantee of getting their money paid back in full.

The bottom line: Bank failures can and do occur. They have, however, become relatively rare occurrences as the economy chugs along. It's wise, however, to at least periodically look at your bank accounts and to understand your deposit insurance coverage situation.

The $100,000 level of deposit insurance is generally applied per person, but, because of the various ways accounts can be structured (single, joint, and more complex irrevocable trust accounts), the FDIC's EDIE is an enormously helpful tool for determining insurance coverage.

Is Your Bank Insured?

Here's a question many of us take for granted: Is my bank insured?

It's fairly simple to check this out when you go to a branch office or the headquarters of a bank. The logo of the FDIC appears on the door of the office and on those little placards at the teller counter or the desktops in the lobby. It becomes trickier to verify this in the online banking world.

What to do? Look at the online bank's Internet home page. Many will feature the FDIC logo or the words "Member FDIC."

READY, SET, STOP: DO YOUR DUE DILIGENCE

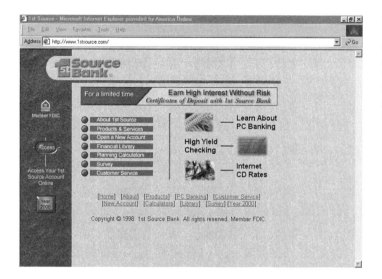

The home page of 1st Source Bank of South Bend, Indiana, features the "Member FDIC" message prominently on the left.

Still not assured that the online bank you're looking at is FDIC insured? The FDIC can help here, too.

1. Open the FDIC home page at *www.fdic.gov*. Note the second item on the left under Deposit Insurance. Click the Is My Bank Insured? question, which is actually a link to a form page.

▼ **Try It Yourself**

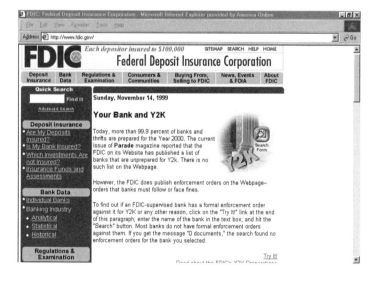

The FDIC's home page offers a link to help you determine whether your online banking institution is insured.

2. In the first text box on the form, type the name of the bank about which you want information. We typed 1st Source, which we scouted out earlier. If you know the bank's home location, type that information in the City and State text boxes. As a challenge, we left these boxes blank. Then click the Find My Institution button.

On the form provided by the FDIC, type the name and location of the bank you want to know more about and click Find My Institution.

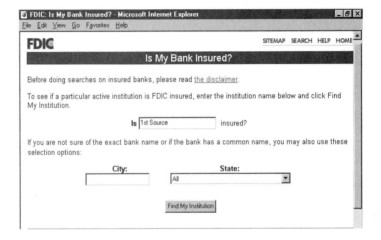

3. A confirmation (or denial) page appears, reassuring you that your cyberbank is insured—or warning you that you should look for another bank. In our search, we found that 1st Source Bank is, indeed, FDIC insured.

The confirmation was quick on the next page. 1st Source Bank is FDIC insured.

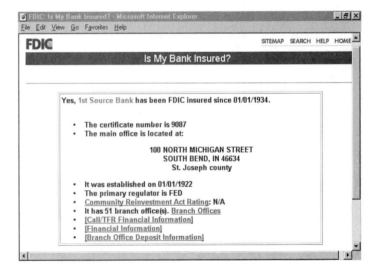

4. You can click the links on the results page to look at additional information about the bank you are researching.

Is Your Credit Union Insured?

We could not find a similar deposit insurance research tool for credit unions. The National Credit Union Administration, the insurer of credit union members' shares (basically equivalent to deposits), provides basic information at its Web site on the topic of share, or deposit, insurance.

This is significant because credit unions are in operations that are not federally insured by the NCUA. Our advice is that you should check out whether your credit union is insured. As you do for banks and the FDIC logo, look for the NCUA logo when you're dealing with a credit union.

If you cannot confirm a credit union or a bank's deposit insurance status, contact the NCUA or the FDIC by email or telephone. Confirming an online bank's regulatory status is an important part of determining its legitimacy as an online bank. Again, do your due diligence.

A Regulatory Who's Who

You might be surprised at how many federal regulatory agencies are directly involved in the affairs of banks, savings associations, and credit unions. There are five, not counting an interagency group. It's good for you as the consumer to know about these agencies because they are good places for you to go with complaints if you think your bank isn't treating you fairly.

The following is a quick tour of the federal banking regulatory agencies and the institutions they supervise:

- The *FDIC* insures deposits at the nation's 10,000-plus banks and savings associations. It is the primary regulator of state-chartered banks and savings associations that are not members of the Federal Reserve System. Web address: *www.fdic.gov*.

- The *Federal Reserve*, the central bank of the United States, was established by Congress in 1913. The Fed regulates bank holding companies and banks that are members of the Federal Reserve System. Another major responsibility that falls to the Federal Reserve is conducting monetary policy (markets can move when Federal Reserve Board Chairman Alan Greenspan speaks). Web address: *www.bog.frb.fed.us*.

- The *Office of the Comptroller of the Currency*, part of the U.S. Treasury Department, supervises national banks. Web address: *www.occ.treas.gov*.

continues

continued

- The *Office of Thrift Supervision*, also part of the Treasury Department, regulates federally chartered savings associations and savings banks. Web address: *www.ots.treas.gov*.
- The *National Credit Union Administration* is the federal agency that charters, supervises, and is the share (or deposit) insurer for federal credit unions and most state-chartered credit unions. Web address: *www.ncua.gov*.
- The *Federal Financial Institutions Examination Council* is an interagency group made up of representatives of the five bank and credit union regulatory agencies. It prescribes uniform principles, standards, and report forms for the federal examination of financial institutions. It also makes recommendations to promote uniformity among all the federal bank and credit union regulatory agencies. Web address: *www.ffiec.gov*.

Now let's get even more complex. The Federal Trade Commission and the Securities and Exchange Commission also have roles in financial institution regulation at the federal level. The FTC's responsibilities regarding banking focus on trade practices. The SEC, as you might have already guessed, focuses on the sale by banks of securities, such as stocks and corporate bonds. As financial institutions continue to develop into one-stop financial services shops, these two agencies likely will have increasing regulatory roles.

In addition, many states have departments of banking or finance that regulate financial institutions chartered by a particular state. These state-chartered banks, credit unions, savings banks, and other institutions must comply with state regulations as well as with one or more federal regulatory agencies.

A Look at Consumer Protection Regulations

In addition to its monetary policy role and the regulator of bank holding companies and banks that are members of the Federal Reserve System, the Federal Reserve has yet another important responsibility: It develops and implements regulations for a number of consumer protections.

These consumer protection regulations include the following:

- Regulation B, equal credit opportunity
- Regulation E, electronic funds transfer
- Regulation M, consumer leasing
- Regulation Z, truth in lending

- Regulation CC, funds availability and collection of checks
- Regulation DD, truth in savings

All these regulations can pertain to online banking, but the two most relevant to this discussion are Regulation E and Regulation CC.

Regulation E governs electronic funds transfers, including automated teller machine transactions and online banking transactions. Basically, the regulation limits a consumer's liability for an unauthorized transaction (say from a lost or stolen credit card) to $50.

Regulation CC establishes a schedule for when deposited funds should be credited to a consumer's account. Before Regulation CC was in effect, financial institutions had widely varying policies regarding "check hold" periods (the amount of time from when a customer deposited a check to when those funds became available). We'll talk about this regulation further in the next chapter.

What You Should Know Now

We've covered the reasons for doing preliminary due diligence on both online and real-world banks and credit unions before making the opening deposit. To recap:

- Periodically review your deposit insurance coverage situation and how it could change in the future. Talk to your banker to get all your questions answered. This is one area where you will come out much better if you know your exact coverage and risks.
- Check your current or future bank or credit union's federal deposit insurance status.
- Understand the role of bank and credit regulators, including the Federal Reserve, in developing consumer protection regulations. Contact these agencies if your bank is not treating you fairly.

PART II
Using Online Banking Products and Services

CHAPTER 6

Begin with the Basics: Opening an Account and More

It's time to get online and see first hand the look of online banking. If you aren't logged on to the Internet, that's OK. We plan to walk you through the basics by visiting a few different banks' online sites.

Each bank site is different, but there are striking similarities. The reason for this is simple. Banks are turning to other companies or third parties to provide the technology necessary to securely bank online. If your bank's online system looks similar to others, that's OK. Many institutions use similar systems to connect their account information and transaction systems to your computer through the Internet.

Although we show you demonstrations of the basics in this chapter, in the next two chapters you will learn some of the more advanced functions, such as bill payment and getting a loan. We call them *advanced*, but once you get into the thick of it, it all takes about the same effort: a few clicks of your mouse.

What You'll Learn in This Chapter:
- How to open an account.
- About other features you'll want to try, such as viewing an account, transferring funds, viewing canceled checks, ordering checks, locating branches and ATMs, downloading information to financial management software, and communicating with email.

> **The Power of Internet Banking: Tracking Your Family's Spending Habits**
>
> A major benefit of online banking is the ability to view transactions as quickly as they are posted to your account by your bank. You can keep track of checks you've written or bills you've paid electronically, as well as debit card transactions and purchases.
>
> For families, such as couple with a joint checking account, the information available online presents an entirely new dynamic. One of us (of course, we won't say whom) returned home one day to his home in Virginia and was asked by his wife about a lunch tab earlier that day.

continues

continued

> She had been online and saw a transaction and didn't recognize the name of what she thought was a restaurant. The only problem: He hadn't made a purchase. It was *her* transaction, and the payee wasn't even a restaurant. The upside: They're still married.

In the Beginning, You Opened an Account

The easiest route to take when you want to start banking online is to stick with your current bank. This way, you don't have to worry about transferring funds into the accounts. The money will already be recorded in the bank's system.

When asking about whether your current bank is online, check to see if it has launched a transactional banking site. Not all banks have fully-functional transactional Web sites where you can actually do your banking. Some banks have sites that only provide you with information. If this describes your current bank, you may need to start shopping around. You should also tell your current bank that you're interested in online banking. You may find that your bank is planning to provide a transaction Web site soon.

A quick note on shopping for online banking products and services: In Chapter 9, "Shortcuts to the Best Deals," we tell you how to get the best deals, the lowest fees, and the best rates.

> **Three Tips to Finding an Online Bank**
> 1. Call your current bank. See if it has a transactional Internet site.
> 2. Go to these bank consumer and consulting sites: Bankrate.com (*www.bankrate.com*), a consumer financial mecca; and Gomez Advisors (*www.gomez.com*), a consumer information site and consultant to businesses.
> 3. Use a search engine such as Yahoo!, MSN, Google, AltaVista, or AskJeeves to check out banks with which you're familiar. In the search bar, type in ***Internet bank*** or the name of a bank you already know and see what you get. We don't think this is the best route because you will hit a lot of non-bank references.

After you've chosen a bank, it's time to open an account. Some banks will let you open your account online and others may still require that you visit a branch to fill out some of the application information. Obviously, it's much more convenient to open your account from your computer online.

Going Online with Your Current Bank

If you already bank offline with the institution, the process is simple and sometimes instant. Banks will provide you with a user agreement online, and you must click the Submit button to indicate that you agree to all the terms and conditions. These documents are long and have a lot of legalese, but they are important to read. They list fees and rates and the bank's guarantee, if the institution has a bill payment function. By indicating that you agree to the terms, you are in essence providing an electronic signature.

Real and Electronic Signatures: As this book goes to press, Congress continues to debate whether electronic signatures carry the same weight as real signatures.

Going Online with a New Bank

If you don't already have an account with the bank, getting online isn't that quick.

Citibank (*www.citibank.com*) lists the types of accounts it offers at its site. You then must complete a pretty simple application that includes your name, address, whether you rent or own, how long you've lived in that location, phone number, birth date, mother's maiden name, first school attended, social security number, employment information, driver's license, credit card number, and passport number.

It's not that difficult, but you might need to collect a few documents beforehand. After you submit the application electronically, you may have to wait a few days to get signature cards in the mail. You mail them back to the bank with a deposit. Then, in two to seven days, your account will be opened and you will receive a Citibank Card. You must have this card number to sign in, along with your personal information number.

Typically, your PIN is sent to you through the mail, although some online banks provide online account access more quickly. Make sure that you understand how your bank will inform you about your PIN or other access features, such as passwords.

WingspanBank (*www.wingspan.com*) has a quick system for opening new accounts. You only have to fill out one application to apply for a checking account, brokerage account, credit card, and bill paying features. You get instant approval, but you can't use it without money. So, you still need to get money into the bank. At WingspanBank there are four ways to get funds into your account:

- You can make your initial deposit by mail (seven to 10 days—faster if you send it by priority delivery).

- You can provide for a direct deposit to the new Wingspan.com account from your employer (or some other source).

- You can arrange a wire transfer of funds (which might involve a fee of $15 to $25 from the other bank).

- You can arrange an ACH collection. In this case, WingspanBank asks the other bank to have the funds transferred through the automated clearinghouse network where it will become available to WingspanBank so it can put the funds in your account. The process takes about two business days.

> **A Word About the ACH System**
>
> If you have your paychecks direct-deposited to an account, your bank is likely receiving the deposit through the automated clearinghouse, or ACH, system. This is also the case if you're a recipient of Social Security checks.
>
> The ACH system provides a fast and efficient means for payments to be made. Some online banks enable customers opening an account to authorize the transfer funds from an account they may have with another bank to the new online bank. This typically is handled through the ACH system. Your online bank will ask for your other bank's routing and transit number, which appears on your paper checks if you have a checking account.

Now for the Meat of Online Banking

After opening an online account, it's time to perform one of the more addictive functions: seeing how much money you have in the bank (we liken it to Scrooge McDuck opening his vault). Let's look at an online account statement with CompuBank (*www.compubank.com*).

BEGIN WITH THE BASICS: OPENING AN ACCOUNT AND MORE

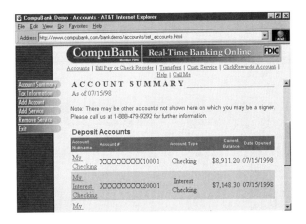

Here is a typical online account report (this one is from CompuBank at http://www.compubank.com/bankdemo/accounts/set_accounts.html). *It has all the basics, including when you originally opened the account, the balance, and the account number.*

We found that CompuBank has created a very user-friendly site. For example, while you view your balances, you can click the Tax Information button on the right side and find out how much interest you've earned on that account.

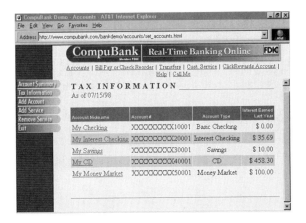

Not all banks provide the interest-earned information as easily as CompuBank's account system does.

View Account Transactions

After reviewing balances, you may want to see account transactions. At many sites, you just need to click the particular account. For example, at the CompuBank site, if you want to see what's been happening in your checking account, click the account.

CompuBank gives you a clear list of recent transactions for a specific account. Here you can see activities, such as which checks have cleared and a recent deposit.

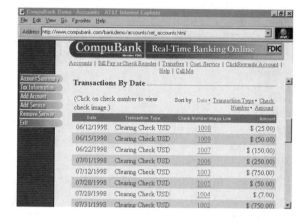

The next feature we'll try at the CompuBank site is pretty special—it isn't offered by all of the banks. It's seeing images of your cleared checks. This function is very helpful. As you can imagine, if your bank only tells you the number of the check that cleared, you have to guess who you sent it to or check with your offline records. With CompuBank's system, you just click the check number to see both sides of the cancelled check.

CompuBank offers this very helpful feature: Click the check number of a check that has cleared, and you can view the front and back sides of the actual check.

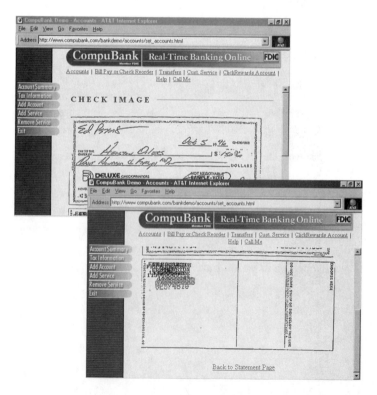

Transfer Funds

Now, to feel the power, let's transfer funds from a checking account to a savings account. To do this at CompuBank, go to the top of the account summary page and click Transfers. On the resulting screen, we want to transfer $100. To do that, we selected the From account and the To account from drop-down list boxes, typed in the amount of the transfer, and clicked the Submit button.

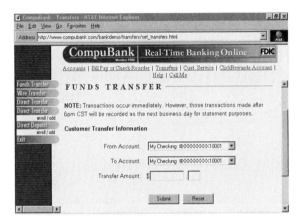

To transfer funds at the CompuBank site, we typed the amount of money we wanted to move and then clicked the Submit button. This transaction, like many online transactions, takes very little typing or input.

After we clicked the Submit button, we could see that the bank had processed the transaction.

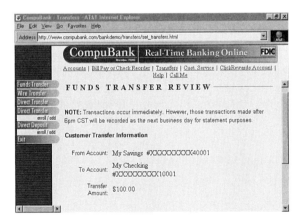

We like the way CompuBank deals with online transfers: at the top of the screen, the bank tells you exactly how it will process the transfer. The transfer is immediate, but if you made the transfer after 6 p.m. Central, it will be recorded as a activity on the next business day.

> **Ready, Set, Go:**
> So how long does an online transaction take you to perform? After you're a pro, that answer varies based on your computer setup, but Citibank estimates that a typical transaction on its site takes about 10 minutes. That "typical transaction" includes signing in, performing a balance inquiry, paying six bills, and then signing off.

> **Real-Time versus Batch Processing**
> There are basically two ways banks operate when it comes to account information. They either operate in real-time or they practice batch processing. In *real-time processing*, you can use your computer to transfer $100 into your checking account and *immediately* see that transfer if you go to an ATM right away.
>
> In *batch processing*, you transfer the funds into your checking account at your computer, but when you go to your ATM later that same day, the checking account balance doesn't reflect the change. This can cause confusion about how much you actually have in your account. Deposits and checks in a batch processing environment typically are updated to your account at the end of a bank's business day.
>
> You should also take note that deposited checks are cleared by your bank and credited to your account based on the type of the check (whether it's written on a local institution and the amount). Your bank can provide you more information about how deposited checks are processed.
>
> If this is a concern, ask your bank if it processes your transactions in real-time or batch.

Download Account Information

Now that you have reviewed the account information and transferred funds, you might want to download your account information into a personal financial management software product, such as Microsoft Money or Quicken. Again, this process is not too complicated with the CompuBank system (or those like it). After reviewing a list of account transactions, you scroll to the bottom of the page where you will find how to download the information. For some general information about downloading account information from a bank site for use in a personal financial software product such as Quicken or Microsoft Money, refer to Appendix B.

BEGIN WITH THE BASICS: OPENING AN ACCOUNT AND MORE 79

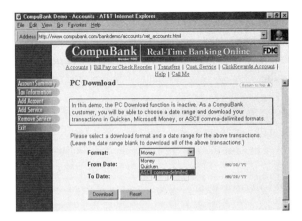

As you can see, to download account information from the online banking site, you don't have to plug in too much information, just what software you have and the dates you want to pull off the site.

Before banking online using Intuit's Quicken product, you must first make sure that your bank supports online banking with this product. Here's how to find out if your bank supports Quicken:

▼ **Try It Yourself**

1. Go to the Quicken Web site at *www.quicken.com*.

2. Scroll down the page. On the left side, under the heading Quicken Solutions, click Quicken 2000 (this is the latest version of Quicken available).

3. Click the Take Me to Quicken 2000 for Windows button (click the other button if you're a Macintosh user).

4. Scroll down the page and click the Frequently Asked Questions link at the bottom of the page.

5. Scroll down the next page to the question, "Which banks or brokerages do you connect with for online financial services…?" and then click the hot link for Participating Financial Institutions.

6. On the next page, you can either search for participating financial institutions alphabetically or by typing in your financial institution's name in the dialog box. If your bank is listed here, you know that you can use your Quicken software to simplify your online banking efforts.

▲

Other Information You Can Obtain Online

We've now shown you some of the basic banking functions, but there are many other added services, such as ordering checks or determining where ATMs or branches are located.

Get Maps of Branch Locations

If you want to learn more about your bank's service area, it may show you a map of its branches. We checked out what Rocky Mountain Bank (*www.rmbank.com*) might show us. When we clicked the About button on the site's home page, we got a map of Montana that pinpointed the bank's branch locations.

Rocky Mountain Bank's site includes a map of Montana pointing out the bank's branches (http://www.rmbank.com/about.asp).

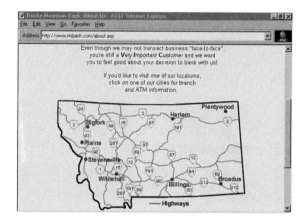

Rocky Mountain Bank, based in Billings, Montana, has done a good job listing helpful information at its site. When we went to *http://www.rmbank.com/contact.asp*, we found the hours of operation, the address, and phone numbers for all the branches.

BEGIN WITH THE BASICS: OPENING AN ACCOUNT AND MORE

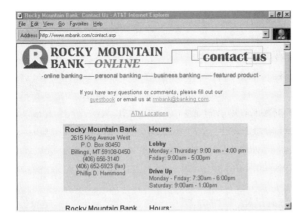

Although this page provides brochure-type information, it sure beats getting it offline by calling and getting stuck in a voice-mail system. (Press 3 if...Press 4 if...Press 5 if...And doesn't that get a little aggravating sometimes?)

Get Maps of ATM Locations

Sometimes locating ATMs can be difficult. And in these times of getting charged a fee for using another bank's machine, it's important to know where your bank's ATMs are located. Chase Manhattan Bank (*www.chasemanhattan.com*) has an easy-to-use ATM locator.

At Chase Manhattan Bank's site, you type in a ZIP code and click Search to see the locations of the ATMs in that zone.

Send Email

There are many other basic features at banks, including sending emails. You may want to send an email to inquire about a fee or about something you've seen on your transaction statement. One word of caution about email—most of the time that we use email, it's not in a secure Internet environment. When you are communicating with your bank via email, don't include sensitive financial data unless you know the system is secure at that point. If you aren't sure, call the bank and ask if its online email is secure.

Order Checks Online

Even though you may be banking online and paying many of your bills online, you're still likely to have a need for good old-fashioned paper checks. Some financial institutions provide consumers the opportunity to order checks online. The check order forms, such as the one at Tinker Federal Credit Union (*www.tinkerfcu.org*), are generally very easy to fill out. There are also non-bank providers of checks, such as Deluxe Corp. at *www.deluxe.com*. You've seen order forms like the one at this site—if you're like us, you get glossy ads for them in the mail several times a month.

BEGIN WITH THE BASICS: OPENING AN ACCOUNT AND MORE

You can order checks online in two ways: directly from your banking institution (as shown here at Tinker Federal Credit Union) or from a third party such as Deluxe Corp.

The Average User Keeps Coming Back

Digital Insight, an online bank consultant for the industry, polled 350,000 online bank customers. The company learned the following about those of us who bank online:

- We log on about 4.6 times each month, slightly more than once a week.
- We average 6.6 account summary inquiries each month and 5.5 account history inquiries.
- We pay about 9.1 bills every month.

"These figures demonstrate that online banking is definitely a 'sticky' application, one that gets customers to return repeatedly," said Paul Fiore, co-founder and executive vice president of new market development at Digital. "Yahoo.com would die for that kind of loyalty."

What You Should Know Now

It's easy to open an account online, but it's not always instant. If you already bank at the institution in the offline world, you usually can start right away. Otherwise, you have to get funds into the account, and that can take many days.

To get funds into an account, it usually takes up to two days if you transfer the money electronically and up to 10 days if you mail in a check or money order.

After you have an account there are many simple tasks to perform including viewing your account, transferring funds, looking at canceled checks or even downloading the information into financial software like Money and Quicken.

Remember you don't have to get lost in voice mail "press heres" any more to get information about your bank. For information about the closest ATM to you or about the hours of a certain branch, check your institution's Web site. Many banks now list this valuable information on their Internet sites.

CHAPTER 7

No Postage Necessary: Paying Bills Online

You thought viewing accounts and transferring funds was a power trip. Now, we're going to take you into one of the most convenient reasons to bank online: Paying your bills from anywhere, anytime, without a single stamp. As the Wells Fargo bank says about its bill payment system: "You're in control. You tell us how much to pay and when, we take care of the rest. It's that easy."

Internet banking has many advantages; when it comes to paying bills, the convenience is pleasantly addictive. You can pay most bills online—whether you owe your baby sitter, the butcher, or the baker.

The person or company you owe doesn't have to be electronically set up to take the payments. You could even tell your bank to send your mom a check once a month. Most banks will simply cut and mail checks for you to the less-technically connected people you owe. The only bills you can't pay online are the ones owed to taxing authorities and the courts. The reason for this restriction is that these institutions usually need additional documentation from you along with what you are paying them. Some banks also won't let you pay alimony or child support using online methods; they don't want to get involved in extra legal matters.

At first you might think that there would be a lot of forms to fill out to get started with online bill payment, but that's not the case. When you are setting up your payee or biller list, the amount of information you need to have is usually limited to simply the right address and an account number, for a credit card or electric bill, for example. The other great advantage is that you can set up recurring payments. You plug in the information once, indicate

What You'll Learn in This Chapter:
- Why paying bills online is addictive.
- How the online bill-paying process works.
- Why you should insist on a guarantee.

Fun Fact:
Jupiter Communications, a New York-based research company, says Americans write 68 billion checks each year. Of those, 18 billion are mailed. A few other Jupiter statistics: 15 billion households will pay bills online in 2002, up from 3 million in 1999.

Save on Stamps:
Let's say you've tracked down a free Internet banking service that allows you unlimited bill payments each month. What can you save if you pay 15 bills a month online instead of through snail mail? If first-class stamps are 33 cents, you'd save $4.95. Over a year, you'd save $59.40. That's not a lot of money, but you never know when the U.S. Postal Service will raise its rates. And that would at least be one or two coffees these days.

So how does a bank make money from this feature? Well, some banks *do* charge you and will limit you on the number of bills you pay each month. When a bank places no limits on you and offers the service for free, the bank is hoping to attract customers who will, ultimately, use other services that will bring in additional fees.

how much and when you want bills paid, and the bank does the rest on schedule. You don't have to dread setting aside a night for bill paying each month!

Some banks allow you to schedule payments one month in advance; others let you schedule them up to one year ahead of time. If you plan to take a trip around the world but you need to make sure that the bills are paid while you are away, this feature is especially handy. Wells Fargo (*www.wellsfargo*), for example, will let you schedule payments for the full year in advance. If you are taking a much shorter trip, First Internet Bank (*www.firstib*) will let you set payments one month before the due date.

If bill paying is the main reason you want to bank on the Internet, we advise that you pick an institution that offers this service for free. There are a wide range of fee schemes for this feature, but the best sites offer free online bill payment with no limits on the number of bills you can pay.

The other factor you should consider when choosing a bank based on bill payment is how strong its guarantees are and whether a bank protects you from bounced, or NSF (for non-sufficient funds) checks and the subsequent charges.

Test Drive Some Bill Payment Systems

There are many reasons to like and to dislike certain bank sites. But if you have ever been bogged down at a site that takes a long time to load, you will welcome an opportunity to go to a page that has a quick response time at the click of your mouse. One bank that we found to be fast was Ohio Savings Bank (*www.ohiosavings.com*) based in Cleveland.

Although Ohio Savings charges $2.95 a month for its bill payment feature, we liked the swiftness of the site enough to make it our first example of how bill payment systems work.

NO POSTAGE NECESSARY: PAYING BILLS ONLINE

The first step to online bill payment is setting up a payee. Most banks have a list of companies and people with which it has partnered and that it can pay electronically (that is, the bank can do an electronic transfer of funds, to the entities on its list). But you don't need to know who's on the list because, ultimately, you will be able to pay almost anyone. After you complete the information about the person or company you want to pay, the bank site will tell you whether that party is on its list of payees. If the person or company is on the list, the bank will send the payment electronically. If it isn't, the bank will simply cut a paper check and mail it.

Free For All:
If you are looking for a bank with free online bill payment and no limits on the bills you can pay each month, Citibank (*www.citibank.com*) might be the online bank choice for you. But check out our list later in this chapter for a few price comparisons.

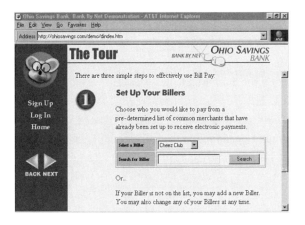

This is the demo at Ohio Savings. As you can see, you don't have to spend a lot of time setting up payments. At this site (as with most banks), you simply need the name, address, and phone number of the person or company you want to pay.

After you have set up a payee with the bank, you can decide to pay your bills to that person or company manually (meaning that you go to the bank's site each month and initiate the payment), or you can schedule the payments to go automatically.

This is the system Ohio Savings provides to set up recurring bills. You can schedule payments weekly, monthly, or up to one year in advance.

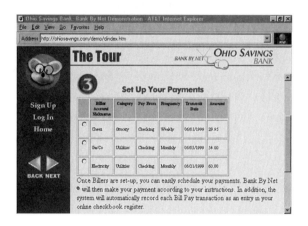

Try It Yourself ▼

Suppose that you want to pay bills at Chase Manhattan Bank (*www.chasemanhattan.com*). It's pretty simple, just as it is at most banks.

1. Log on to Chase Manhattan Bank at *www.chasemanhattan.com* and click Payment. A bill payment screen appears, giving you several options. Click one of the options, depending on the task at hand: one time payment, repeating payment, cancel payment, change payment, payment history, pending payments, add payee, edit payee, delete payee, or review payee.

2. For this exercise, click Add Payee. At this point, you have a little work ahead of you: You must note the name of the payee, give the payee a short name (also called a nickname), account number, address, and telephone. You also indicate whether the payee is for personal or business purposes. Then click the arrow at the end of this list.

3. *Voila!* You get a glimpse at the online file you've just created.

4. This payee is now ready for instant payments anytime in the future. You'll never have to fill out all that information again.

When Does the Money Leave Your Account?

The trickiest part of bill paying online is understanding when the money is taken out of your account. There's a big difference in the approaches used by the real and virtual worlds. When you pay bills through the mail, you send a check to the person you owe and the money isn't taken from your account until the check is cashed or deposited. This isn't the case in the cyberworld.

When you tell your bank that a bill is due on a certain date, the bank will calculate when it must initiate the transaction. Let's say that you owe your brother $10 on January 1. Ohio Savings will take the money out of your account four business days in advance and begin the process of paying your bill. If the bank can make the payment electronically, it will take the funds out of your account two days before the bill is due.

At most banks, if the payment is electronic, the transaction will take two days. But, with a lot of the banks that actually have to cut and mail checks, we found that they take the money out of your account anywhere from five to seven days before the bill is due. The date the money is taken from your account is called the *processing date*. In reality, however, the money is taken out *the night before the actual processing date*. For example, First Internet Bank of Indiana takes the funds out at 9 p.m. Eastern Time one night before the processing date. This is an important detail to know because you can make changes, stop, or alter the payment up until then.

Although paying bills online is an easy process, it still means that you have to have money in your account. Each bank will handle situations involving non-sufficient funds differently. If you have established a recurring payment but don't have enough funds in the account one time, some banks will just not pay the bill—and not even notify you. That's why it's smart to check whether your recurring bills are being paid by going to the bank site and clicking the list of paid bills. In this same circumstance, other banks will pay the bills and charge you for non-sufficient funds. That service could cost you up to $25 per transaction at some banks.

First Internet Bank of Indiana has a good system in place. If you have an overdraft account, the bank will simply pull the money

The Automated Clearing House as Middleman in Your Online Transactions:

When you are reading about your bank's bill payment feature, you will find that some banks indicate that they transmit and receive ACH funds. What this refers to is the handy work of the Automated Clearing House network. ACH is a nationwide batch-oriented electronic funds system that provides for inter-bank clearing of electronic payments. The American Clearing House Association, the Federal Reserve, the Electronic Payments Network, and Visa act as ACH operators or central clearing facilities through which financial institutions transmit or receive ACH entries.

Basically, the ACH system is the middle guy when banks transmit funds to one another.

Ask for Overdraft Protection:

Not everyone has overdraft protection. You have to request it when you sign up for a checking account. If you have a tendency to have more outgoing funds than incoming in your account every once in a while, this is a good feature to request.

from there. If you don't have overdraft protection in place, the bank will not process the payment, nor will it charge you for non-sufficient funds. However, First Internet Bank of Indiana will place a message on your Current Payments screen, indicating that your payment failed because of non-sufficient funds. As is true with most banks, if the payment fails the first time because you didn't have enough money in your account, the bank will not try to pay the bill again, and you must manually initiate the payment.

As we've been repeating, all institutions don't treat cases of non-sufficient funds in the same way. It pays to investigate the policies an online bank has regarding this situation. Netbank, for example, says that it can charge you overdraft penalties for not having enough money in your account to pay a designated bill. Further, the bank warns that you could incur a $25 fee from them and another fee from your payee.

Check Out Your Bank's Bill Payment Summaries

After you have set up your payee list and any recurring bill payments, what other functions can you perform when paying bills online? You can view your account transactions to see whether your bills have been paid on time. You can view the list of upcoming recurring payments you have scheduled. You can make simple changes to your payee list or even cancel future payments. There's a lot of power you can harness with an online bank's bill payment system.

At Citibank, one of our favorite features of its bill payment system is the ability of customers to see total payments made to certain payees. This feature can help you get a good assessment of how much you paid your credit card in one year or how much went to paying off your student loan. Being able to summarize your payments to any single entity can come in handy if you are having a dispute about how much you've paid someone. Without going to the bank or calling anyone for help, you can pull this report together on your own.

The personal financial management software products Quicken and Microsoft Money also enable users to track payments to certain parties or by category of payment. Online banking providers have taken a similar approach in providing such power-searching capabilities. These features put more of your financial management into your own hands. In days gone by, to identify a series of payments to one person or company, you would have had to sit down with a teller and pore over ledger books. Now you can point and click online or in a personal money management software package.

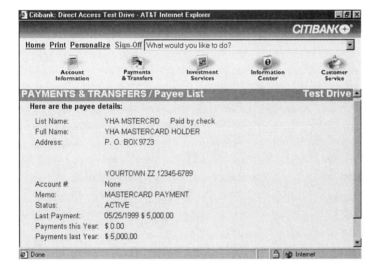

This demo page at Citibank shows how much you've paid a company in the current year and in the past year. This page provides you with a complete history of your relationship with this payee.

Citibank, which offers its online service and bill payment feature free of charge, has a system that is simple to navigate and offers several easy to read, helpful screens.

This helpful Citibank page shows the customer his or her future payments pretty clearly. If there is a problem and he or she want to stop or change a payment, he or she simply click the payee's name.

So he or she clicked one of the payees and got this easy-to-read screen. This page allows the customer to make quick edits to the payment—stop a future payment or change the amount.

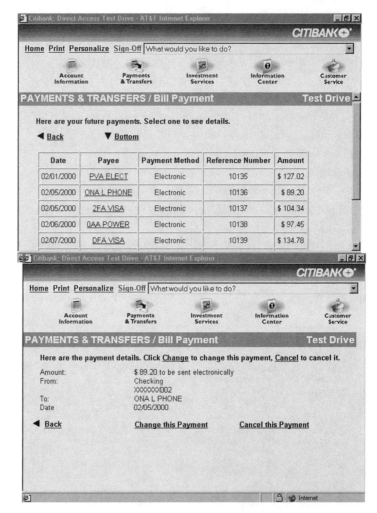

What if the Online Payment System Fails?

We've described a pretty rosy scenario when it comes to bill payments online. But what if there's a glitch in the system? What if a payment doesn't get to your biller or payee on time? Who is to blame?

The Killer App: Bill Presentment

In this chapter, we're giving you the ins and outs of online bill payment, but there's another feature under development that's about to take center stage. It's something called *bill presentment*. This is when companies send you bills electronically instead of through the mail. The financial services world and merchants are trying to figure out the best way to make this happen on a widespread basis.

This service is currently available at a few non-banks online, but as we went to press, there were still many kinks to work out.

One non-bank offering this service is the MoneyCentral offered by MSN.com. MoneyCentral offers a limited service: you will receive bills from only a few select merchants participating in this feature with MSN. The day we logged in, there were only 32 e-billers listed. For example, Con Edison of New York was one of them. That won't do you much good to you if you live in Louisiana.

Here are just a few of the questions being asked about this system: Should the bills be sent to you through your bank? Should merchants send bills to you through your Internet service provider? Should the merchant just send bills directly to you?

Banks, of course, want the bills sent to you through them. If merchants bill you through the banks, this will further ensure that you will use that bank's online bill payment service. That's why some bankers and financial service providers believe that bill presentment is the killer application. If they get this feature on their systems, it will practically ensure that you will use them, and not a non-bank competitor, for bill presentment and bill payment.

Look for the Guarantees

If you want to know what happens if a payment isn't made and it wasn't your fault, you need to check out each bank's guarantee. These policies are customarily listed behind a Terms and Conditions button.

We reviewed several guarantees and found that the best sites have established aggressive strategies to set the record straight for you if the bank failed for some reason to make a payment. Problems do occur sometimes—whether there is a system breakdown at your bank or with your bank's third-party processor. Remember that you may do business with a certain bank, but your financial institution has likely outsourced this function to another company.

Online Resources & Communications, one of these third-party providers based in McLean, Virginia, has challenged the entire industry to maintain "airtight consumer bill pay guarantees." What does this mean? The company will pay unlimited late payment fees and penalties if the biller does not receive properly scheduled bill payments on time. With an Online Resources system, the customer also is protected from paying non-sufficient fund penalties. With this system, the consumer is notified about the problem and given a chance to deposit funds so that the payment can be made.

Many of the guarantees are similar, but it's best to always read your bank's terms and conditions. Most banks won't come to your aid if your account does not contain sufficient funds, if the processing center is not working and you've been notified of that fact, if the payee mishandles the payment, or if you made mistakes when naming the payee or listing its address.

We liked CompuBank's terms stating that it "guarantees that any errors made by its vendors or staff in regard to bill payment will be rectified. CompuBank (*www.compubank.com*) further guarantees to pay any late fees associated with payments that arrive late."

Hibernia Bank (*www.hibernia.com*), based in New Orleans, also has a few reassuring words: "Hibernia will reimburse you (up to $50) for any late fee or penalty you incur and work with you and the payee to resolve any issues associated with a delayed payment."

Shop 'Til You Find the Right Price

If bill paying is the main reason you want to bank online, it's smart to shop around for an institution that offers this service for free. There are a few banks out there that offer free bill payment, but most have some complicated charging schemes.

Here is a look at how much it costs to pay bills online. We've gotten prices from some giant, regional, and small banks, as well as a few Internet-only institutions to help you determine what's right for you. All these fees are subject to change.

Flagstar Bank (*www.flagstar.com*), based in Bloomfield, Michigan, provides online banking with bill payment free of charge for the first six months. After that period, online banking is $4.95 without bill payment; with unlimited bill payment, the banking service is $8.95 a month.

Citibank (*www.citibank.com*) has made it simple: Online banking is free of charge and so is unlimited bill payment.

Wells Fargo (*www.wellsfargo.com*) offers bill payment for free if you keep a combined monthly balance of $5,000 in your personal checking and savings accounts. If you don't maintain that balance, the bill payment service is $5 each month.

Washington Mutual Savings (*www.washingtonmutual.com*), based in Seattle, Washington, has no basic charge for banking online but does charge $5 for unlimited bill payment each month.

First Tennessee Bank (*www.ftb.com*), based in Memphis, charges a $10 setup fee for most customers (except for students and "priority choices" account holders), no monthly fee for online access without bill payment, but $5.95 with this service. For the first two months, you can get bill payment for free.

Ohio Savings Banks (*www.ohiosavings.com*), based in Cleveland, charges $2.95 a month for unlimited bill payment.

Wingspan Bank (*www.wingspan.com*), an Internet-only bank, offers free unlimited bill payment to its customers who have a combination of checking accounts, certificates of deposit, installment loans, credit cards, and investment services. For other customers, the fee for bill payment is $4.95 each month for the first 10 transactions. After that, each payment is 25 cents.

CompuBank (*www.compubank.com*) another Internet-only bank, offers free unlimited monthly payments.

What You Should Know Now

Not all banks offer the same bill payment features. Check out the demos offered on the bank sites to see what systems you like best.

If you pay a lot of bills each month, it's a good idea to shop around for banks that offer the service for free. They are out there—keep searching.

Read your bank's "terms and conditions" statement. There you can get the details about what the bank will guarantee if their system breaks down and your biller doesn't get your money on time.

CHAPTER 8

Beyond the Basics: Cool Add-On Products and Services

Banks are offering a lot more today than they were just one or two years ago. That's the beauty of online banking: You can perform the traditional functions, such as depositing money and transferring funds, but you can also buy other financial products—including insurance and securities—from the comfort of your home, 24/7. Investment firms are entering into the banking business, and banks are entering into the investment world. The lines between all these different types of financial institutions have been blurred.

Banks are also offering their loan products, services, and credit cards online. After you've tried these functions over the Internet, you might not want to ever fill out an application with pen and paper again.

One word of caution: Americans have traditionally thought of the money we've deposited in banks as safe and secure. But if you opt to make an uninsured investment in a product such as a mutual fund from your banking institution, you need to know that such a securities investment is not insured by the Federal Deposit Insurance Corporation. We're reminding you of this harsh reality; when you enter into one of these circumstances with a bank, the bank will also remind you.

In this chapter, we will provide you with an overview of a few financial products being offered by banks online. In Chapter 9, "Shortcuts to the Best Deals," we'll give you several tips on how to get the best deals on these products and services.

What You'll Learn in This Chapter:
- ▶ All about online loans and credit cards.
- ▶ How banks get into the investing and insurance businesses.
- ▶ How you can involve the federal government in your banking investments (hint: buy a U.S. Savings bond online).

A Loan in a Matter of Minutes

Banks aren't anxious to give away their money, but they are using computer programs that allow them to determine your credit risks and to issue you a loan in a matter of minutes over the Internet.

Banks operating on the Internet are buying software systems that enable them to offer loans to people who have never set foot inside their doors. For example, one company, The Forms Group, is marketing to community banks a basic Web online banking solution with a function called ZipDecision. With this add-on, banks offer their customers real-time decision-making on loan applications. The process takes into account a customer's credit history, or credit score, and the institution's lending policies.

The Forms Group's ZipDecision product provides a means for financial institutions to offer online loan applications with decision-making capabilities on their Web sites. For example, a customer would enter information on a secure credit application and submit it electronically to the bank. The ZipDecision software applies the bank's credit criteria to render a decision on the loan.

> **Credit Scores**
> What's credit scoring? Credit scoring is a system used by banks and others to determine if you are a good loan risk. The process takes into account your credit experiences, your bill paying history, the number and types of your accounts, collection actions, late payment history, and outstanding debt. This information is processed into a computer program that compares your credit performance with that of consumers with similar profiles. The result of this comparison is a total number of points—your credit score—that helps banks predict your credit worthiness.

Loans from Online Credit Unions

Let's look at one institution: a credit union that offers a quick loan approval service. Most of the sites we discuss in this book are banks, but we wanted to highlight the services of at least one credit union. Although credit unions offer competitive rates and fees, they also are off limits to many of us. Credit unions limit their customer base to the members of its organization. Legally, they are supposed to serve only those members. But if you can join a credit union (through the company where you or your spouse may work), you should check out what it has to offer. Credit unions are offering online services, just as banks and thrifts are doing.

With that said, let's look at the loan service of Security One Federal Credit Union (*www.sofcu.org*). This institution is open to "anyone who lives, works, worships, or goes to school in Arlington, Texas." It's likely that your financial service provider will offer loan services similar to those from Security One.

Banks and Thrifts:
The term *thrift* typically has described a savings institution, but there really is no practical difference between a thrift and a bank.

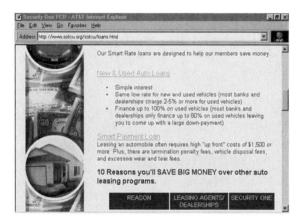

This screen shows all the types of loans that Security One Federal Credit Union offers to its customers. The drawback to a credit union is that you have to be a member of a specific group before you can qualify for any of its services.

After you submit your information, it could take as little as two minutes to learn if your loan has been approved. If the loan isn't approved online, you are encouraged to contact a loan officer using the old-fashioned method of the telephone or an in-person visit. As is true for all credit unions, you must provide some proof of membership in the credit union before you can be approved for an online loan.

Fun Fact:
Americans will obtain 8.9 million loans and credit cards over the Internet by 2003, according to Forrester, an online research and consulting firm. Additionally, Forrester estimated that in 1999, eight percent of online consumers turned to the Internet for mortgage information.

Loans from Online Banks

Let's look at another institution's online lending service. Rocky Mountain Bank (*www.rmbank.com*), based in Billings, Montana, allows you to apply over the Internet for several consumer and residential loans. The Rocky Mountain system isn't instant. After you fill out the application, you have to print it out and mail or fax it to the bank.

The latter point is important. If time is important to you, you'll want to investigate how long it will take for your "online" loan application to be processed. In some cases, it can occur in real-time (minutes or less). More complex loans, such as home mortgages, will likely take at least 24 hours or more.

Rocky Mountain Bank's system is pretty easy to navigate. Here is its special mortgage center, where you can apply for a loan or get a pre-qualification.

Rocky Mountain Bank also makes interest rate comparison easy for its customers by including this rate chart on the first page of its mortgage center.

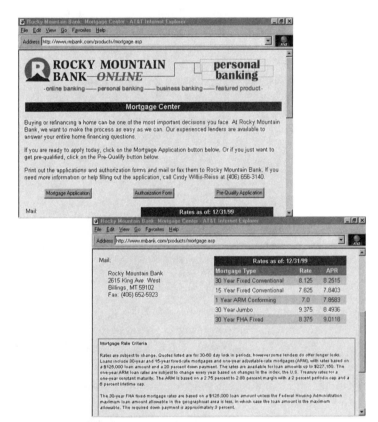

Telebank (*www.telebank.com*), based in Arlington, Virginia, was one of the more user-friendly sites we found for getting loans. This bank makes it easy to apply online for an auto loan or mortgage. It has partnered with E-Loan (a mortgage loan portal) to provide home loans and with People First Finance (a consumer loan portal) for its auto loans.

What did we like in Telebank's mortgage center? It provides a payment calculator so that you can figure your payment for different loan amounts, interest rates, and amortization terms. It provides an amortization calculator so that you can determine the breakdown between your principal and interest payments. It allows you to get pre-qualified, and it will recommend the best loan in your area based on your situation. The E-Loan database contains more than 50,000 mortgage loans from 70 lenders. In a matter of seconds, the site will show you the best available loan rates that day.

Unlike most online financial institutions, Telebank's mortgage center is a portal to multiple mortgage loan providers. Most institutions taking online loan applications will subsequently fund those loans.

You can apply online for loans at the Telebank center. The company estimates that it takes about 20 minutes for you to fill out the loan application. You don't get instant approval, but a loan consultant is supposed to call you within 24 hours. That same loan consultant will work with you until the closing.

The biggest selling point for going to Telebank to get a mortgage loan through E-Loan may be that you might be able to save some money. E-Loan estimates that its loan process is $1,500 less expensive than using an offline loan agent. One caveat: A low interest rate on a mortgage loan does not always mean the best service. It pays to shop around and to talk to others when considering a mortgage loan. Another caveat: Pay attention to the rate-locking features of any mortgage loan. An advertised low rate today may be higher tomorrow.

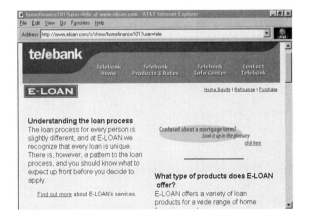

We especially liked the Home Finance 101 site provided by Telebank and E-Loan. Here you can read the questions of other customers, see the answers, and learn about several mortgage terms such as "good faith estimate."

When we linked to E-Loan from the Telebank site (E-Loan's direct Web address is *www.eloan.com*), we found a glossary of mortgage terms that proved tremendously helpful. We learned all about amortization. They defined two terms in the following manner:

> amortization—The repayment of a mortgage loan by installments with regular payments to cover the principal and interest.
>
> amortization term—The amount of time required to amortize the mortgage loan. The amortization term is expressed as a number of months. For example, for a 30-year fixed-rate mortgage, the amortization term is 360 months.

Review Your Credit Report

You also can order copies of your credit reports off the E-Loan home page. Three companies, Experian, Trans-Union, and Equifax keep records of our credit histories. Banks use these reports to determine whether we are safe risks for loans. It's a good policy to review your own credit report now and then, especially when you are about to apply for an important loan. E-Loan allows you to request a report online from Experian—and receive that report within 30 seconds —for $8. It will mail you reports from all three of the companies for $29.95.

> **What Are Credit Reporting Agencies, Anyway?**
>
> We don't like to think that anyone is keeping track of our personal lives, but it's true that certain aspects of your life are being monitored. For example, three credit reporting companies are tracking your financial histories. And they aren't just tracking you, they are giving that information to your bank.
>
> The following are the three major credit bureaus and their contact information:
>
> - *Equifax*—P.O. Box 740241, Atlanta, Georgia., 30374-0241, (800) 997-2493
> - *Experian*—P.O. Box 949, Allen, Texas, 75013, (888) 397-3742
> - *Trans-Union*—760 West Sproul Road, P.O. Box 390, Springfield, Pennsylvania, 19064-0390, (800) 916-8800
>
> When you contact one of these agencies, they must give you all the information they have on you, and they must tell you who has requested your report within the past year (two years for employment-related requests).

These agencies must provide free reports to you if you are unemployed and plan to look for a job within 60 days if you are on welfare or if your report is inaccurate because of fraud. Also, if a company took adverse action against you because of a report, you are entitled to one free copy within 60 days of receiving the disappointing notice. If none of these scenarios work for you, by law, the agencies can charge up to $8 a copy when you request your report.

If you get a report and spot information that isn't accurate, the agency has a responsibility to make proper corrections. If you want more information about credit reports, the consumer division of the Federal Trade Commission (the government's best kept secret) has several articles that can help you. To learn more, go to *www.ftc.gov* and click the consumer protection section.

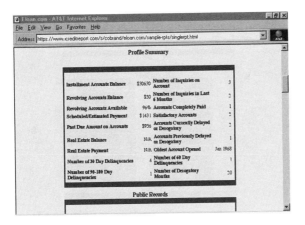

This is a sample page from a demonstration credit report on E-Loan's Web site at www.eloan.com. This is just one page of information; credit reports can contain many pages and be pretty comprehensive. If you never have checked on your reports, do so soon.

Applying for Credit Cards

Credit card deals are abundant in the online world. Advertisements for low-interests credit cards are splashed across many of the bank sites and on search engines and Web hubs. Although you are probably bombarded with credit card applications in your offline mail boxes, the Internet allows you to shop around for good deals on your own. Because the competition is hot for your business, watch out for the low *teaser rates* (the attractive interest rates offered to you for an introductory period before much higher rates apply).

Applying for credit cards is made easy at many sites, but the feature that will bring even more convenience into your busy life is the ability to view your account balance and other information

Shop for Your Banking Service: If there is one point we want to emphasize, it's this: Shop around for your banking services. According to the Credit Union National Association, Americans spend more than $25 billion a year on fees for checking and bank cards—about $250 for each household.

online. Citibank (*www.citibank.com*) allows its basic banking customers, as well as non-customers, the opportunity to view and pay their credit card accounts online. With this service, you can check account activity, your credit limit, and when your next payment is due. If you are a Citibank customer, you simply use the bank site's Direct Access online service. If you aren't a customer, you use the site's Account Online feature.

Citibank offers several different credit cards and makes it easy for you to apply on the Internet for any one of them, whether you have an account at the bank or not.

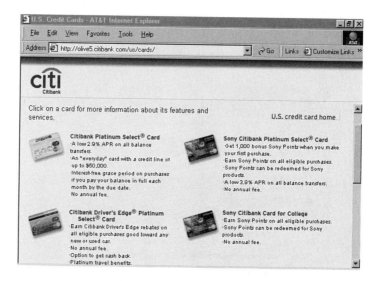

Try It Yourself

1. To apply for a credit card from Citibank, go to the institution's home page at *www.citibank.com*.

2. Under the Personal Financial Services heading, click Credit Cards. Then, at the bottom of the subsequent page, select the United States as your country and click Go.

3. At the top right of the new page, under Apply for a Card, click Go.

4. Click any of the card products presented to learn more about their features.

5. From any of the specific card product pages, click Apply Now, which appears on the left side of every page.

6. Fill out the application and wait for your new card to arrive in the mail!

Investing and Buying Insurance Online

Along with account products (such as checking and savings accounts) and loan products, online financial institutions are branching out to offer customers additional products and services. These new products include investments and insurance.

Investing in Stocks and Bonds Online

At many of the online bank sites, you can click your way into a financial service center (think of it as a virtual bank lobby that can lead you to all manner of financial services products). Net.Bank (*www.netbank.com*), for example, has partnered with the discount brokerage, UVEST Investment Services. You can buy stocks online and have your trading fees deducted from your checking or money market accounts.

WingSpan Bank (*www.wingspanbank.com*) has an extensive investment service (click Brokerage at the top of WingSpan's home page). WingSpan Investment Services offers many products, including an extensive line of securities. There's no charge for accessing this service, but when we went to press, a trade was $19.95.

This is the first page of WingSpan Investment Services, a subsidiary of WingSpan Bank. This page gives you quick access to quotes and market news.

Fun Fact:

Forrester reported that of the 28.6 million online households in the United States, 1.4 million were trading over the Internet.

Bank of America (*www.bankofamerica.com*) offers an investment service that we found easy to navigate. Products offered include mutual funds, stocks, and options offered through Banc of America Investment Services, Inc., brokerage account information, company research, market data and news, and real-time quotes.

As an aside, note that in the name *Bank of America*, the word *bank* is spelled with a *k*. In the name *Banc of America Investment Services* (which provides investment products), the word *banc* is spelled with a *c*. Welcome to the wild, weird world of bank and banc holding company nomenclature.

If you are a novice to the world of trading stocks, you may be under the impression that the average Joe or Jane can't trade stocks unless he or she has a broker. The truth is that you can buy stock from anyone; a stock broker just connects buyers and sellers of shares of publicly traded companies. The online investment services act as that go between for you and the stock market.

If you want to learn how to trade online, Bank of America has a good demo that you can use to test your skills.

Try It Yourself

1. Go to Bank of America's home page at *www.bankofamerica.com*. In the upper-right corner of the screen, click the Learn More button under Online Investing.

2. Scroll down the page and click the Demo of Discount Brokerage Services Online Trading Capabilities hot link.

3. Use the demo to research a particular company's stock. How about Microsoft, Incorporated (which has the NASDAQ ticker symbol MSFT)?

4. Begin takeover of Microsoft (we're just kidding).

BEYOND THE BASICS: COOL ADD-ON PRODUCTS AND SERVICES

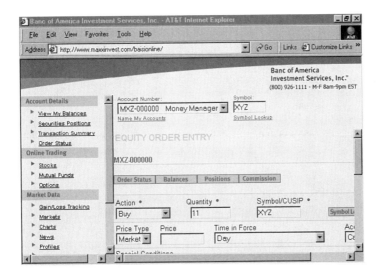

Banc of America's investment service page is where you go to buy or sell stocks. Notice the customer service number in the upper-right corner you can use if you are having problems or have a few investing questions.

Buying Insurance Online

The next non-bank product we want to discuss is insurance. In using the word *insurance*, we're referring to the gamut of insurance products, including auto, life, home, health, and business, as well as insurance products that are also investments, such as annuities.

The Telebank site (*www.telebank.com*), mentioned earlier in this chapter, makes the process of shopping for insurance online simple. Telebank's insurance center is affiliated with The Insurance Answer Center. Although you can't actually buy insurance online, you can learn about rates and then make a call to a service representative, 24 hours a day, to make the purchase.

Some of the best features of The Insurance Answer Center include free quotes, a dictionary of terms, and an online storage vault where you can keep your policies and copies of your insurance applications. You can obtain a myriad of policies from this site and its representatives, including auto, home, life, and annuities.

This is what your My File page might look like at The Insurance Answer Center. It's an excellent way of keeping track of some of your insurance paperwork.

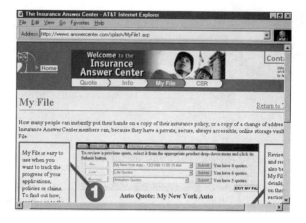

PNC Bank (www.pncbank.com), based in Pittsburgh, Pennsylvania, offers an insurance service that works in cooperation with Ins Web Corporation. With Ins Web Corporation, as with many online insurance centers, you can fill out one form and receive multiple quotes. This site also offers a learning center, called "Financial Peace of Mind," that could come in handy if you need to know more about insurance products.

Insurance shopping has never been this easy. Your options are available 24/7, and these sites help you shop around for the best rates.

Keep in mind that it's not just banks marketing insurance online these days. Insurance agencies and insurance companies are providing online insurance quotes. To see what's out there, type *online insurance* in any Internet search engine's search box.

Buying Savings Bonds Online

Everyone is getting in on the act of e-banking and e-investing. The U.S. government is no exception. By logging on to the U.S. Department of Treasury's Web page, you can purchase savings bonds over the Internet.

As investing tools, savings bonds have always been a safe bet; now they are a 24-hour service. You no longer have to go to a bank or credit union to buy the bonds. Go to the Department of Treasury's Web site at *www.treas.gov*, click Sales and Auctions, and you are moments away from investing in U.S. savings bonds. Loaning money to the government has never been so easy.

BEYOND THE BASICS: COOL ADD-ON PRODUCTS AND SERVICES

In addition, the interest rates on savings bond are competitive with other bond investments, with the added security of the backing of the full faith and credit of the U.S. government.

The process of buying the bonds is simple and quick. The government site presents several pages that explain all the different bonds. Then you simply buy what you want using your Visa or MasterCard. You can buy up to $500 in bonds during each online transaction.

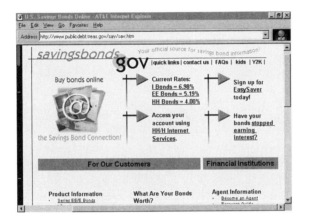

This is one of the Web pages the government uses to explain how much Series EE bonds will cost you.

When you arrange to buy bonds online, the paperwork (that is, the amount of computer input you have to do) is limited. You fill in your name, address, Social Security number, and a beneficiary (if you choose to include one). After you input your information, the site shows you what the actual bond will look like with your name printed on it. You can have the bond sent directly to you or to a friend or relative, if you are giving it as a gift.

> **Buy Bonds to Bail Out the Government**
> Most of us buy bonds because we know they are safe investments and offer good tax breaks. But the bottom line on U.S. savings bonds is that they help the government deal with its debt. In that spirit, after you buy a bond, you can click the Bureau of Public Debt Web page and check to the penny how much the government owes on any given day. When we checked on the figure in the fall of 1999, it was a whopping $5,696,176,434,485.80. To review our nation's debt today, go to http://www.publicdebt.treas.gov/opd/opd.htm.

What You Should Know Now

Getting a loan doesn't have to take days or weeks. At some online sites, it takes only minutes. The Internet also makes it simple to apply for credit cards and to keep track of your purchases from your own computer.

Banks aren't what they used to be. They are offering a variety of products, including insurance policies and securities.

Even the U.S. government is in on the online financial services game. It allows you to buy U.S. Savings bonds at the U.S. Department of Treasury Web page.

CHAPTER 9

Shortcuts to the Best Deals

It seems like cruel and unusual punishment that we didn't start with this chapter, but we wanted to explain some of the basics before you got here. The better informed you are about Internet banking, the better consumer you will be, with or without cheat sheets from a few online-savvy advisors.

There are companies who want to help you out with your search for online banking products, and they offer this service free of charge. We can't list them all, but in our search, those we found to be most helpful were Gomez Advisors, which rates and compares online bank sites; Bankrate.com, which offers you a monster amount of information on the best deals going on credit cards, home loans, certificates of deposits, and a long list of other products; and Financenter.com, which also includes information about the best financial services deals on the Internet.

In this chapter, we will also explain how an online calculator can help you make up your mind about several financial questions that might be haunting you, and show you how you can save some dough by shopping online through your bank's home page.

What You'll Learn in This Chapter:
- You can surf for hours, or you can just go to the online consumer help sites.
- Where to find the best deals in online banks.
- What's an online calculator?
- Some banks are hot-linked to your favorite stores.

Gomez Advisors: A Powerhouse of Advice

Gomez Advisors (*www.gomez.com*) works both sides of the fence. It advises companies on how to better get your business while you shop or bank online, and it provides consumers with rankings of a host of merchants in the e-commerce world. It will also link you to a few good deals each day and provide you with some basic consumer information

> **You Can Stay on Top of the Trends**
>
> Gomez, which calls itself "The eCommerce Authority," has a lot of good statistics and basic information to share with you to make you a smarter online bank customer and shopper.
>
> From the Internet Banking Division's Web site, we learned that "by an 82 percent to 56 percent margin, Internet-only banks were more likely than branch banks to respond promptly and accurately to phone and email customer service inquiries about banking and about Web offerings.... Internet-only banks are also much more likely to help customers apply for new products with Web-enabled applications and tend to be more adept at coordinating their Internet offerings with ATM networks in real-time."

Gomez advises consumers on several topics. It will tell you about the best sites selling automobiles, and it will enlighten you about online auctions. We, of course, are interested in how Gomez can help you pick an online bank.

Try It Yourself

1. Open Gomez's first page on banking at *http://www.gomez.com/channels/index.cfm?topcat_id=1*. There's a lot to choose from. We found the Overall Score link at the top of the page and the Compare Online Banks section at the bottom of the page to be the most helpful tools.

There's a lot of information on Gomez's first page about banking. Explore the links or click directly on the Overall Score link.

2. Click the Overall Score link at the top of the page. The Internet Banker Scorecard page opens. Here you can see how Gomez ranks a raft of online banks. Click Bank Scorecard Methodology at the bottom of the page if you want to see the criteria by which the banks were judged.

SHORTCUTS TO THE BEST DEALS

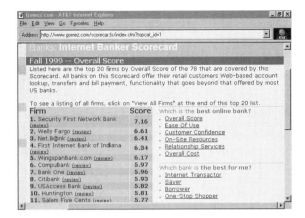

Gomez's Internet Banker Scorecard is a great place to go if you are starting from scratch in your search for an online bank.

3. Click the name of a bank in which you are interested to see a description of the services and then link directly with the bank.

4. Back on Gomez's first page on banking, you can scroll down to access the Compare Online Banks area. Select two banks from the drop-down list boxes provided and click Compare to see a page that compares these two banks. This tool is a handy way to conduct a side-by-side comparison of two banks that you may be considering.

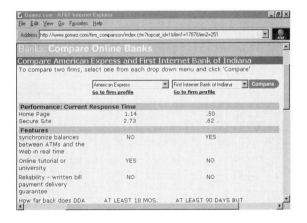

Gomez's Compare Online Banks feature lets you choose two banks you want to compare; it then shows you a page like this one to help you with your choice.

If you are always in a rush and speed is important to you, Gomez can show you how fast a bank's pages will download onto your screen. From the Internet Banker Scorecard page, select the bank you're interested in and then click the Bank Performance Monitor link to see how your bank ranks in this area.

Although Gomez doesn't rank all the banks in the country, it does include in its survey all Internet bank sites with more than $2 billion in deposits. It uses more than 100 criteria to rate the sites, including whether the bank guarantees on-time bill payment and whether the bank allows customers to submit loan applications over the Internet.

We don't think you should use Gomez exclusively as you pick your bank, but you can see that the features this company offers certainly will be a big help to you. Two additional sites that can help you sort through the hundreds of online bank options available are described in the following section.

Find Your Best Rates

As you've seen, Gomez Advisors can list a few good deals in the banking world each day. However, other sites also specialize in helping you shop around for all sorts of banking products. We found two that were easy to use: Bankrate.com and Financenter.com.

Bankrate.com

Bankrate.com (*www.bankrate.com*) has been online since 1995. It's produced by the same company that publishes the *Bank Rate Monitor*, a newsletter for banks and consumers. At first, the site is overwhelming because of the amount of information it presents, but if you have the time to spend with it, you are sure to learn about a few good deals. Overall, Bankrate.com gives you rate information on 51 products, including mortgages, certificates of deposits, and money market accounts from about 4,000 financial institutions around the country. The following three figures show some of the many informational screens available at *www.bankrate.com*.

SHORTCUTS TO THE BEST DEALS

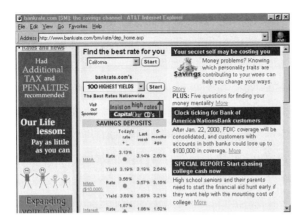

These are the top five deals on one-year certificates of deposits on the day we checked the Bankrate.com site. The data is updated every weekday night.

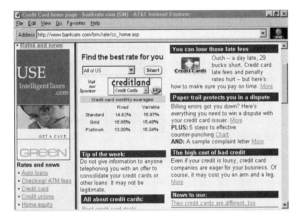

This is what we learned about credit card rates at Bankrate.com. The page includes a lot of good details that can help you make a decision about where to apply for your next piece of plastic.

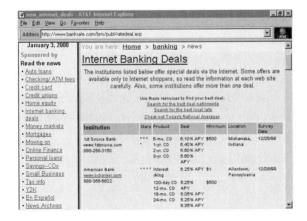

Bankrate.com's Internet Banking Deals page gives you another way to compare online bank sites and what they offer by comparing rates on a few of their products.

The site also includes several helpful articles to keep you informed about trends in banking. While we were there, we learned the following interesting bits of information:

- 64 percent of the banks online offer an online banking service for free.
- The average cost for online banking is $5.44 a month.
- 25 percent of the banks online don't charge for their electronic bill payment service.
- It costs a consumer about $94 a year if he or she has a checking account and does not maintain a balance that would make the online banking service free.

One of our favorite features of this site was the Get Rates pull-down option. This function allows you to compare rates on a variety of products offered by banks in the city of your choice. In addition, the Internet Banking Deals link provides another source you can use to compare what's out there, and the High Five link leads to a page that lists the top five deals on any given day on a variety of products.

Bankrate.com claims it uses journalistic standards as it collects its data and makes its suggestions. We definitely got the feeling that the site was fair and reliable. It also has a strong pro-consumer tone.

Financenter.com

Financenter.com sprang from a company that originally marketed home equity loans on the Internet. Today, it partners with businesses to promote their products in exchange for compensation. Some of the deals are worth checking out. In addition, the site provides basic information about finances.

Although you can use the Financenter.com site to shop for good deals in credit cards, savings accounts, and so on, our primary interest in this site is the 110 calculators the company makes available through its ClickCalcs link. The company also places these calculators on other sites. Banks can buy software from the company to place these calculators on their sites. When you, the consumer, use these calculators at a bank site, it's a seamless function. You aren't even aware that Financenter.com is involved. When we went to press, Financenter.com had its calculators on about 150 sites on the Web. Don't know anything about online financial calculators? The next section helps you out.

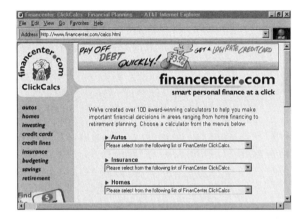

Although Financenter.com has a friendly site, the best part of the site is ClickCalcs, a link to 110 calculators offered by the company.

The Calculator Is Your Crystal Ball

The online calculator is one of the best added values a bank can put on its site. It's a tool you can use to help make decisions based on your own personal information. Banks hope these tools motivate you to open a savings account, invest in a certificate of deposit, or buy any one of their services. There are calculators that can tell you which Roth IRA is best for you, how much life insurance you might need, the impact of different interest rates on credit cards, whether a new or used car is better for you, whether you are better off retiring, and what it will take for you to become a millionaire. Let's take a tour with a calculator provided by Financenter.com.

1. Open the Financenter.com home page at *www.financenter.com*. Click the ClickCalcs link at the bottom of the page to open a new page that has a list of all the types of calculators the company offers.

2. Click the Millionaire link to open a form page. This page is actually the calculator; you answer the questions by filling in the blanks. As you can guess, changing the values you enter in these blanks affects the outcome.

▼ **Try It Yourself**

With this calculator, you can find out what it will take to become a millionaire (in our case, about a million dollars). Type in the numbers based on your life and click for the answer.

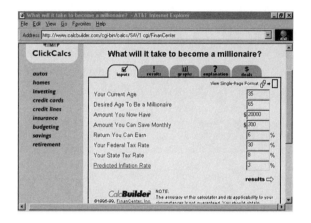

3. Click the Results button to view the calculated results for the values you entered. Click the Inputs tab at the top of the page if you want to change any of the values you entered originally. Click the Graphs button if you want to see graphics depicting the likelihood of your becoming a millionaire any time soon.

The news returned by the online calculator isn't always the best, but at least you know now. We'd better save a little more if we want to become millionaires before age 96.

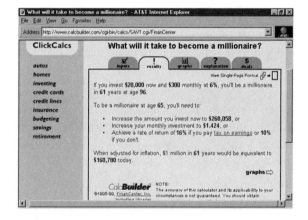

Shop Till You Drop

Banks are always looking for gimmicks (such as the calculator) to get you to return to their sites. One of the growing new services is the virtual mall. Smaller banks are posting hot links to the merchants in their own towns, further establishing themselves as a connection to the local community. In essence, these online banking sites are bringing the traditional town square to the cyberworld.

Other banks are partnering with nationwide merchants to bring a large variety of items and services together in one shopping area. They are also offering discounts and guarantees. Chase Manhattan, which has a very user-friendly site in many regards, has a pretty extensive marketplace.

The Chase Manhattan site at *www.chasemanhattan.com* offers a large virtual shopping mall. On top of that, the company will give you discounts if you buy items from selected merchants and use your Chase credit or debit card. Why go straight to the merchant's shop when you can go to your bank first and save a little money?

You can go straight to Chase's online mall by clicking *www.chaseshop.com*. Here, the bank offers you discounts and customer service to help you shop without hassles. We also liked the free ground shipping offered on the night we went to the site. In all of our surfing, we found that Chase had the most extensive and helpful cybermall.

> **The Community Bank Connection**
>
> Community banks are known for offering a few good deals. But many of them are too small to appear in the lists at the sites that rank online banks, and they have too few dollars to market themselves to you.
>
> When we went to press, we were awaiting the launch of Bankzip.com. This site is a one-stop shop for customers looking to bank online with a community bank in their area. Bankzip.com is also supposed to offer a nationwide network of surcharge-free ATMs.
>
> Pennsylvania-based Patriot Bank Corporation developed Bankzip.com, an Internet banking network. Consumers type in their zip codes when they arrive at the site; the site then transfers the customer to a bank in the network that has laid claim to that area. Banks will be charged a $25,000 admission fee to be included in the site's list of resources.
>
> Bankzip.com won't guarantee that you are getting the best deal, but it will be another source to use as you look for an online bank.
>
> Community banks that decide to join this service will have the benefit of a national marketing campaign and back-office support, including loan origination and servicing and a call center that enables Web customers to call for assistance.
>
> Why might a local community bank be a good bet for you as you pick an online bank? At some point, you might want to actually meet your banker. If you opt for an online bank far away or one that is Internet

continues

> *continued*
>
> only, you will be destined to bank only in the cyberworld. You will have no human touch, except perhaps over the phone. If you pick a community bank, you have the option to walk into a branch at some time. A possible downside to a community bank is that it may not have a lot of money to spend on the latest technology.

What You Should Know Now

In this chapter, you've learned about some shortcuts to finding an online bank and about some hot gimmicks that banks are using to entice you to their sites. The following is a review of what you should have learned:

- There are a few "cheat sheets" on some Web sites to help you analyze what bank is best for you, including Gomez Advisors (*www.gomez.com*), Bankrate.com (*www.bankrate.com*), and Financenter.com (*www.financenter.com*).

- Take advantage of calculators. Most bank sites have them, but if yours doesn't, go directly to *www.financenter.com* to test drive a few.

- Online banks are offering discounts on cybershopping expeditions if you shop from their sites and use their credit or debit cards. A few online banks also offer guarantees. Your bank is a good place to start when shopping online.

CHAPTER 10

Attention All Small Business Owners

As a consumer, online banking gives you more immediate control and management of your personal finances. In essence, it helps you do your job better as chief executive officer of You, Inc. by making your financial information available to you anytime, anywhere, through the power of the Internet.

If you're the owner and manager of a small, or large, business, online banking can help you do your job better as the CEO of Your Business, Inc. Banks are reaching out to business customers through online products and services including business checking accounts, loans, and cash management.

We'll look at some of the products and services banks are offering online for businesses, and will also provide you with some tips to consider for online business banking. You'll see some similarities with online banking product and service offerings for consumers and businesses—such as checking, loans, and savings account products—but there are some differences.

What You'll Learn in This Chapter:
- What products and services are available.
- How to shop for online business banking services.
- Security issues you must address.

What's on the Menu?

Online business banking products and services include business checking accounts, loans, savings accounts, and more sophisticated products, such as sweep account arrangements. A *sweep account* enables a business to earn interest on excess funds on deposit in transactional accounts.

Business Financing Services

Online business banking products and services include financing, such as credit lines, term loans, real-estate secured loans, and loans guaranteed by the Small Business Administration. Zions Bank of Salt Lake City, Utah, provides business loan applications online at its Web site (*www.zionsbank.com*).

Zions Bank provides both online consumer and business banking services. Many banks that are offering online banking services offer products and services geared to consumers as well as to businesses.

Zions Bank provides business owners a complimentary "Capital Resource Guide" when they submit an online business loan application to the bank.

Bank of America (*www.bankofamerica.com*) also provides online applications for loans and financing, as well as a "Business Center" featuring information and resources for businesses. To access the Business Center, Bank of America requires you to register. *Be careful here.* Bank of America is likely prospecting for potential business customers, so be ready for a phone call, a letter, or an email when you sign up.

Business Checking and Savings Accounts

Online banking services for businesses also include business checking and savings accounts. These services are similar to their online consumer account counterparts. They allow a small business owner to track account balances, payments, and deposits, as well as make payments electronically through online bill payment or directly through the automated clearing house network.

As we've discussed in earlier chapters, the fees for bill payment services can and do vary. You'll want to include such fees, if there are any, on your comparison-shopping checklist.

The online account services offered to business patrons may also include payroll and payroll tax preparation. Bank of the West (*www.bankofthewest.com*) promotes this feature among its online business banking services.

Integrated Banking for Businesses

One of the major benefits of online banking for businesses is the ability to integrate a variety of financial management activities and to track them online through a secure Internet connection.

Merchant services, such as the electronic submission of daily credit card receipts, are another valuable benefit of online business banking. How so? Let's say that you own a retail gift shop and submit your credit card receipts to your bank through your electronic payment terminal at your cash register at the end of each business day. The next morning, you could go online to your business bank to quickly confirm the deposit of those credit card receipts.

> **Fun (but Frightening) Fact:** One-third of new businesses fail within six months, and three-fourths of business start-ups shut down within five years, according to the University of Virginia's McIntire School of Commerce.

Wells Fargo Bank (*www.wellsfargo.com*) is one of the standouts in marketing this integrated approach to business banking. The institution's Business Gateway provides "...the power to see transaction history, transfer funds, view the detail of any deposit, pay federal business taxes, and much more, right from your own PC."

At one of Wells Fargo's Web pages (*http://wellsfargo.com/biz/demo/demoStart*), you can test drive the institution's Business Gateway.

Wells Fargo's online Business Gateway services include transferring funds between accounts, setting account balance warning screens for individual accounts (the bank describes this as a fuel gauge for an account), paying federal business taxes online, and initiating stop payments and ordering checks.

The Business Gateway also allows business owners and managers to monitor all transactions, assign access rights to an accountant or employee, and view detailed lists that can display each check in a deposit.

Here's the opening page of Wells Fargo's online business banking demonstration. From this page, we clicked the Account Balances hot link...

...and got a look at the overall status of accounts. Note the similarities between the look and feel of this program and consumer online banking systems illustrated in earlier chapters.

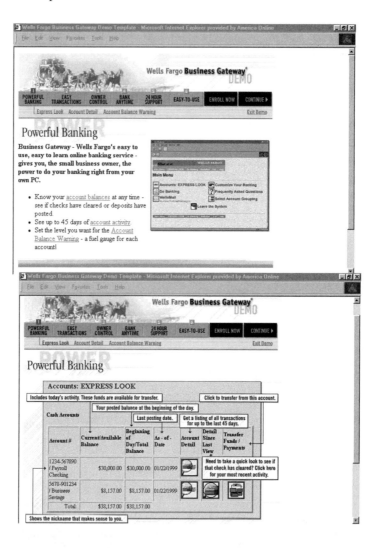

Cash Management Features for Businesses

Cash management is another example of how the technological melding of a bank's back-office data processing and the Internet can help small businesses increase revenues by earning interest on otherwise idle funds. The Federal Reserve Board's Regulation Q prohibits the payment of interest on business checking accounts and is one of the last vestiges of interest-rate regulation on the part of the government.

Banks have learned to get around Regulation Q through *sweep* accounts in which a business' checking account funds are swept each night into an interest-bearing account. This maneuvering is somewhat complex and, many banks argue, completely unnecessary.

These banks and their trade associations would prefer that Congress simply eliminate Regulation Q through legislation. In the meantime, sweep accounts remain the primary way for businesses to earn interest on their money.

Through online banking, a business can determine how much cash should be swept out of its checking account and into an interest-bearing savings account at some point during the day. Those funds can earn interest until the business decides it needs the cash for upcoming expenses, at which time the funds are swept back into the checking account.

GrandBank of Maryland explains the mechanics of sweeping succinctly in its page on Business Checking at its Web site (*www.grandbank-online.com/bbcheck.htm*). "Earn interest on excess funds with an automatic 'sweep of funds' from checking to savings," the bank says. "Simply set the minimum amount of funds to be maintained in your checking account and we'll do the rest."

Chittenden Bank of Burlington, Vermont, provides a look at its online business banking system through a series of demo screens on its Web site (*www.chittenden.com/demotest/intro.html*).

Chittenden Bank's online business banking demonstration shows how users can navigate the system's cash management and transaction features.

Similarities in Online Banking for Businesses and Private Customers

As we mentioned earlier, there are many similarities between consumer and business online banking products, services, and features. Philadelphia-based Pennsylvania Business Bank provides an interesting side-by-side comparison of the benefits of online banking for consumers and commercial customers at its Web site (*www.bizbank.org*).

As we've noted elsewhere, many of the online products and services for consumers and businesses are similar, as Pennsylvania Business Bank explains in its comparison. For businesses, one of the primary benefits of online banking is cash management—the ability to track and monitor accounts and account balances, and to quickly put idle funds to work earning interest.

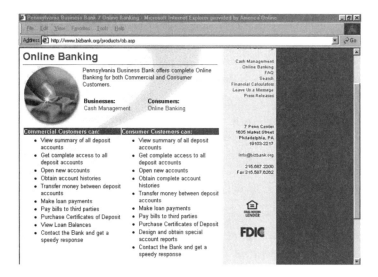

Here's Pennsylvania Business Bank's comparison of the benefits of its online banking services for consumers and business customers.

Finding an Online Bank for Your Business

Our advice to private consumers in Chapter 4, "Choosing Your Bank," on shopping for an online bank is also helpful for business owners looking for Internet banking services. As with shopping for a consumer online bank, we would encourage you to first take a first at your current bank's online business banking services.

By moving to online business banking through your current bank, you'll avoid the hassles of changing banks, which can be complex if you've got loans or lines of credit and use other banking services. For example, if you're a retailer, your new bank will likely need to be able to provide merchant processing services to enable you to accept credit and debit cards for payments. You may also need courier or other cash-handling services.

Many small businesses will be geographically limited when shopping for online business banking services. If you're taking in cash from customers, such as a restaurant or retail store, you're going to need a local branch to make your end-of-day or end-of-week deposits. Obviously, if you handle physical cash, a bank that exists only in cyberspace is not for you; you need the physical presence of a teller window and a deposit box.

Take a look at your current business banking provider's lineup of offerings. Also consider what services you'll need from online business banking. Ask your account representative for a demo, or schedule a meeting to learn more about your bank's online services and how they fit the needs of your business.

If you're going to have to shop around for online business banking services, you'll need to carefully compare features and fee structures. Most online business banking sites we visited offer a variety of accounts with fees that vary depending on average balances kept at the bank.

This is a common practice. Business banking, also known as *commercial banking*, is typically priced by a bank based on the concept of "account analysis." What this means is that a bank looks at a business's average deposits and transaction volume and applies this analysis in the form of a credit against fees charged for account maintenance and other business banking services. This makes fee comparison a tricky venture, so keep that in mind when considering taking your business to a new bank.

Here's another way to look at it. A bank earns interest on the money you have on deposit by using those funds to make loans or other investments. However, it costs your bank to provide you with checking account and other services. *Account analysis* is a phrase that describes how your bank gauges what it earns and what it costs to handle your business accounts. If your business maintains high average balances or a steady flow of deposits at the end of each business day, your business likely will have lower fees.

One way to learn more about what other business owners are doing online through their banks is to network with your peers. We suggest your local chamber of commerce as a good resource. If your bank offers online business banking, talk to other business owners who are online and using those services.

A Word About Security

We're going to examine online banking security issues in more detail in the next few chapters, but if you're a small business owner, you've got some additional security concerns that you'll want to address before banking online.

One issue is account access. You'll want to make sure that you can establish levels of access to your business's online accounts. This is not much different from your deciding who can write checks on your business checking account. Maybe the only person with that access level is you. However, if you have an accountant or bookkeeper, you'll need to consider what level of access that person will need to all your online accounts.

Wells Fargo's online business services allows business owners to establish three levels of account access privileges: Do Banking, View Only, and No Access. For those employees who have full access to "do banking," you, as the owner, will want to impress upon them the importance of keeping passwords and other information confidential and secure (we'll give you some common-sense security tips in upcoming chapters).

Richmond County Savings Bank in New Jersey describes the access-setting features of its online business banking services in a FAQ on its Web site at *www.rcbk.com*. The bank's system enables business owners to restrict access to specific functions, reports, and accounts. Special profiles can also be created to allow confidential information to be shared among those with privileged access (such as accountants and managers).

The bank also notes that business owners can export their account information to financial management software such as Quicken, Money, or QuickBooks.

SunTrust Bank of Atlanta provides a demo of its online business banking services using QuickBooks through its Web site at *www.suntrust.com*.

1. Go to *www.suntrust.com*. Under the SunTrust Online heading, at the upper-left of the home page, click PC Banking for Business.

2. A new page opens. On the upper-right side of the page, click the word Demo under the QuickBooks logo.

3. Follow the directions on the next page for loading the QuickBooks demonstration. This may take some time.

4. Try the various options after you've loaded the demo. The demo is a good way to get an idea of QuickBooks' capabilities.

Attention QuickBooks Users:
Intuit, the maker of Quicken personal financial software, also produces the popular small business accounting software products called QuickBooks and QuickBooks Pro 99. If you're a Quickbooks user and are considering online banking services for your business, you'll want to check out how your online bank's system works with this business software.

▼ **Try It Yourself**

> **For Starting a Business**
>
> Maybe you don't need online business banking services just now because you're still thinking about how to start up a business. There's help available on the Internet.
>
> The Small Business Administration provides information about starting a business, as well as how to obtain financing. The SBA, as it is called, is a government agency that provides loan guarantee programs and other services to assist small businesses. Its Web site address is *www.sba.gov*.
>
> Another good source for information about starting a small business and electronic commerce is the U.S. Business Advisor, which is maintained by the SBA on behalf of several federal agencies. The address is *www.business.gov*.
>
> An Info Desk button is available on the home page of the U.S. Business Advisor that provides online information about small businesses including business plans, Web links, assistance and training, government publications, business development, financial assistance, laws and regulations, and e-services. The site also has links to the National Fraud Information Center, which provides information on Internet-related fraud and the Better Business Bureau.
>
> The U.S. Business Advisor even offers an Internet tutorial covering topics such as email, teamwork, finding information, and a parent's guide for safe and effective use of the Internet. The tutorial is available from a hot link at the bottom of the U.S. Business Advisor home page (click Learn the Internet).
>
> A good private-sector Web site to learn more about starting a business is American Express' Small Business Exchange (*www.americanexpress.com/smallbusiness*). The Small Business Exchange offers advice on buying or selling a business, day-to-day management, finding financing, business insurance, cash management, and other key topics.
>
> The American Express site also offers tips on creating an effective business plan, including a Try It Yourself section (hey, we love those!) in which you can test your management skills by helping a hypothetical bakery, Bella's Biscotti, get up and running.

Going Beyond Banking

Although they're emphasizing online integration of all of the financial service needs of a business, many banks are also helping their business customers get on the Internet and conduct e-commerce, as well as establishing communities of Web-based businesses and merchants.

Bank of America, with its Business Center, and many others, including Wells Fargo and SunTrust (*www.suntrust.com*) are using their Web sites to help small businesses by acting as information resources as well as financial services providers.

Some institutions are even using their Web sites to provide virtual town squares or shopping malls to link consumers and businesses, and businesses with other businesses, online. The concept is based on the idea of a virtual community that brings together businesses or consumers with common needs.

Suppose that you're in the business of making widgets. Through your online bank's town square or shopping mall, your specialty is highlighted for other consumers and businesses to see. In other words, the town square virtual community provides another avenue for businesses to market their products and services, whether they are widgets, wedding cakes, or consulting services.

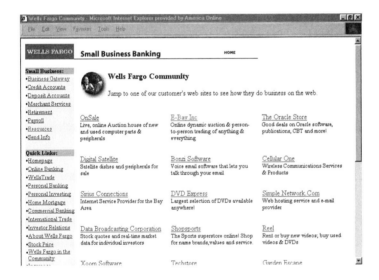

Wells Fargo promotes Web merchants through hot links from this page on its Internet site. There are some big players here, including eBay and OnSale.

What You Should Know Now

In this chapter, we've covered the basics of online business banking as well as provided guidance for shopping and adopting online banking if you're a business owner. The following are some reminders:

- The products and services offered to businesses are similar to online banking services offered to consumers, including viewing accounts and transactions online, paying bills electronically, and transferring funds. Look at your business's current banking needs, as well as possible future services, to determine how you can benefit by interacting online with your business bank.

- If you use a business accounting software product, such as Intuit's QuickBooks or a financial management product such as Quicken or Money, check with potential online business banks about how their systems will work with your management software.

- Our advice for finding an online business bank is similar to what we've recommended for consumer online services: Look locally first and find out what your current bank offers. Be careful when comparing fees for online business banking because of the wide variety of accounts and services available. Talk to your business bank's representative and ask for a demo of online business banking.

- As a business owner, you'll have some unique security issues you'll need to address as you go online with your business banking. If you have employees, such as accountants or bookkeepers, will they have full access to your business' online account? Check with your online business bank about appropriate controls to ensure security and to control who can access the financial information.

PART III
The Facts About Security and Privacy

CHAPTER 11

Trust Is More Than a Word

In the early to mid-1800s, banks provided a safe place for people to store money or gold. Banks had huge, heavy safes or vaults where cash and other valuables could be kept. This was quite literally a safer option for people than hiding money in a mattress, burying it somewhere, or carrying it around.

In addition, banks offered to pay customers interest in exchange for the use of their funds on deposit. Even with inflation and the time value of money factored in, this was an attractive option. However, there were risks. These were the days before deposit insurance, when banks often went…well, bankrupt. In such instances, depositors of failed banks were left high and dry without their funds.

In those days, what would it take to encourage someone, say your great-great grandfather, to keep his money in a bank? Probably not a higher rate of interest. Your forebearer might suspect that a high-rate-paying bank was "gambling" with depositors' money.

The inducement was, in a word, *trust*. Today in a banking context, "trust" most often means services such as estate planning and other fiduciary activities, but it still carries a powerful connotation of entrusting a third-party (the bank) with your money. Banks have worked hard to live up to this expectation.

So much and so little has changed. Today, of course, federal deposit insurance protects consumers' deposits in insured banks and credit unions, as discussed in Chapter 5, "Ready, Set, Stop: Do Your Due Diligence." That's a big change from the banks in frontier life.

What You'll Learn in This Chapter:
- ▶ All about security and the Internet.
- ▶ What the online banks are promising you about how secure they are.
- ▶ What the government's role is in Internet security.
- ▶ Why the issue of security should be a shared responsibility.

However, banks still "buy" our money from us in the form of interest on our checking account deposits, savings deposits, and certificates of deposit. In turn, the banks "rent" our money to other customers in the form of loans—for education, homes, business ventures, credit cards, or other purposes. Although we may sound like Jimmy Stewart in his speech to depositors in *It's a Wonderful Life*, we're getting to a point: Money and credit are the lifeblood of the American and the global economy, and the issue of trust remains very important.

The Internet and Security

The issue of trust extends to online banking over the Internet. In fact, it could be argued that online banking has grown slowly, even as the Internet exploded in recent years. Why? Because financial institutions were willing to wait until issues such as security had been more clearly addressed by this new and very low-cost delivery system.

Jumping to provide online banking in the early phases of the Internet's evolution would have meant risking the trust that banks have earned from their customers. Instead, most banks tackled the Internet in stages, beginning with a simple Web site (now somewhat derisively called "brochureware") and then moving on to provide more advanced products and services.

The financial services industry has also formed organizations and groups that work together to help ensure the security of the Internet as a place to do banking business and conduct e-commerce. One such organization is the Banking Information Technology Secretariat, or BITS, which we will tell you more about in Chapter 14, "A Security Checklist."

"Security has been a high priority since BITS' inception because without security, there will be no e-commerce," says Catherine Allen, chief executive officer of BITS. Allen is not alone in her view about the high regard financial services providers have for security on the Internet.

A New Realm

The explosion of the Internet and e-commerce over the past few years has challenged financial services providers along with many other businesses and industries.

One major challenge for banks is simply keeping up with the latest technological innovations and industry practices. The Internet is such a new delivery mechanism for products and services that many financial institutions lack the internal resources, or technical skills, necessary to adapt to the new medium.

In response, financial institutions are partnering with third-party providers of technology resources and solutions in their quest to better serve customers through the Internet and online banking.

These third parties provide online banking software that links a financial institution's data and information resources to customers through the Internet. This is why you'll notice, as you shop for online banking services, that two banks' online sites may look and feel quite similar. If so, the chances are the two institutions are using the same online banking software interface to provide customer access to account information.

"Technology is now the key driver in the delivery of financial services," says Matt Chapman, chairman and chief executive officer of Concentrex Inc., a technology provider to the banking industry. "This means that financial institutions need assistance to keep up; even the largest institutions will need to rely increasingly on external providers."

"New entrants into the financial services market can succeed based on superior technology, and many long-time players won't survive because they won't keep up," adds Chapman. "In this environment, innovation in the delivery of financial services will depend largely on developing and deploying the underlying technology that drives that delivery, together with the necessary industry and regulatory knowledge to make the technology work."

To look at this another way, online banking requires a broad range of technological services in form of hardware, software, and expertise. A bank will likely need to shop for a third party to provide the necessary software and interfaces to provide online services—in a secure environment—to its customers.

What Are Banks Promising?

Many financial institutions that provide online banking services are up front in informing consumers about Internet security and in answering consumers' possible questions to help ease their concerns.

When you click a link on the home page that asks "Concerned about security?", Lyndonville Savings Bank (www.lyndonville.com) of Lyndonville, Vermont, provides this security statement.

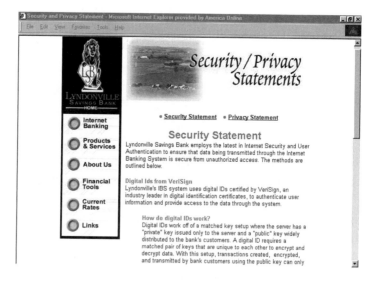

Some Good Examples of How Bank Sites Explain Security

Busey Bank (*www.busey.com*) of Urbana, Illinois, provides a sterling example of explaining Internet security to consumers:

> "You probably often write a check at a store or to pay a bill," the bank says. "Consider the information printed on your check that is easily read by anyone processing that check—your name, address, phone number, bank name and account number, and perhaps your driver's license number or Social Security number.
>
> "In contrast to this printed information which anyone can read, the information that travels across the Internet using a secure Web banking system like ours, is encrypted (scrambled) according to a complex mathematical algorithm. To unscramble the data, someone would have to have both the ability to 'crack' this algorithm plus many, many hours of computing time on a super-computer."

Stillwater National Bank & Trust Company of Stillwater, Oklahoma, does a very good job of explaining the three general categories of Internet security on its Web site at *www.snb-ebank.com*. The three categories are

- *Log-in protection for the user*—This is when you use a password and login I.D. to begin an online banking session. It also includes security features such as "three strikes and you're out." This feature allows a user three chances to log in for an online banking session and guards against a "brute force" hacking attempt in which passwords are randomly and repeatedly attempted (more on this in Chapter 12, "The Dark Arts: Cryptography and Encryption").

- *Transmission security*—This security category involves methods to ensure information security between your computer and its Web browser software and your online bank, such as encryption and decryption. (*Encryption* means encoding a message; *decryption* means decoding it. We'll cover the specific techniques in Chapter 12.)

- *Server security and information privacy/integrity*—This security category includes security techniques to protect a bank's information from outside threats. These techniques include firewalls, separate computer servers, and filter routers.

Busey Bank provides a Security FAQ link on the right side of this page on its Web site. When we clicked it...

...we arrived at a series of informative questions and answers about online banking and Internet security.

Fun Fact:

In the 1940s, a number of children's radio shows, such as *Little Orphan Annie*, closed with a secret message to the listening audience that could be deciphered with an official decoder ring. Most decoder rings featured the alphabet and the numbers 1 through 26 on two different rings. For each show, the narrator would tell the audience the correct ring setting for that episode, such as A-10. A series of numbers was read off, which then could be decoded and turned into letters of the alphabet using the ring. And so, a generation of cryptologists was born.

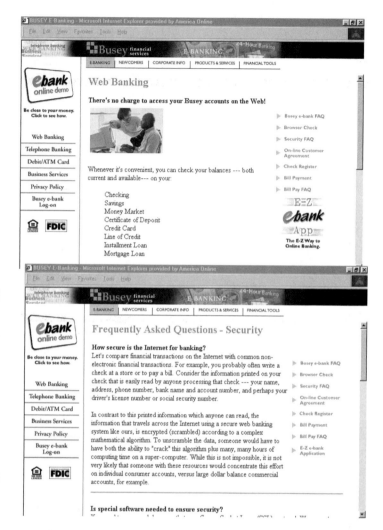

We're going to get into the mechanics of encryption in the next chapter, but we very much like Busey Bank's plain-language response to the question, "How secure is the Internet for banking?"

We also like the bank's admonition to customers at the bottom of its security FAQ page. "Remember: Do not give your user I.D. and password to anyone," the bank warns.

TRUST IS MORE THAN A WORD

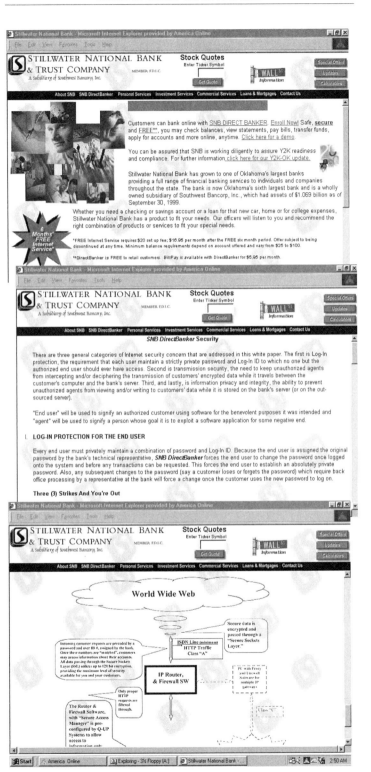

Stillwater National Bank & Trust Company (there's that word again, trust) highlights the word "secure" on its home page. We clicked it...

...and arrived at this page providing details on "three general categories of Internet security," including log-in protection, transmission security, and server security and information policy/integrity.

Scrolling down the same page, we arrived at this chart illustrating Stillwater National Bank's various security measures and practices. This is probably more than most people need to know, but it's still good to see and a nice example of providing information for technologically inclined customers.

First National Bank and Trust of Pipestone, Minnesota, provides a Security button on the left side of its home page. Note the prominent placement of the FDIC logo and the Equal Housing Lender logo, as well as the graphic concept of a "drive-through on the Information Superhighway."

Clicking First National Bank & Trust's Security button took us to another solid explanation of online banking security issues and measures. Like the preceding example from Stillwater National Bank, First National's Web page also has an illustrative chart depicting the flow of communications between the bank and its online customers.

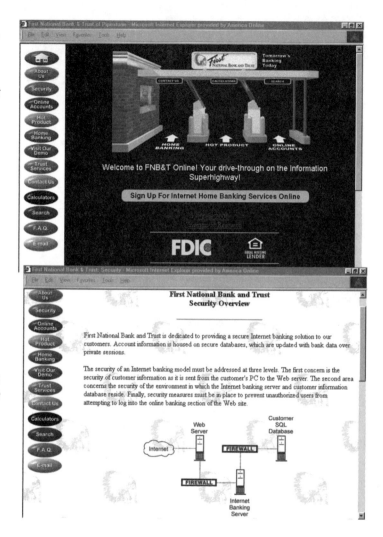

How Banks Are Protecting Themselves Against the Terrors of the Internet

Online financial services providers are employing a number of protective measures to guard themselves against hacking. These steps were highlighted by Peter A. Browne, a senior vice president of First Union Corporation, who testified with Catherine

Allen of the Banking Information Technology Secretariat before the House Banking subcommittee:

> "It is important that you appreciate the extensive measures that banks and other financial institutions have in place and continually improve in order to assure the security of our systems," Brown told the congressional panel. "This is historic and has, if anything, increased in importance with the addition of the Internet environment."

Online banks, said Brown, are doing the following to heighten security:

- Using updated virus scanning software packages on all file servers and PCs.

- Ensuring that all network connections are properly secured.

- Ensuring that desktop modems used by employees are secured and properly registered.

- Using real-time, inbound scanning systems for electronic mail and attachments.

- Educating customers and employees not to download files from unknown origins.

- Implementing broad-based customer and employee education.

- Employing strong password processes and controlling password changes.

- Masking customer account number information from online banking screens.

- Providing a timed log-out feature on online banking sites.

- Providing remote access security systems for those employees and business partners who dial in to corporate networks.

- Conducting periodic tests of security from the viewpoint of someone trying to hack in to an online bank site.

We're going to cover many of these topics in the next chapter, but we mention them here to underscore how seriously financial institutions view Internet security.

The Government's Role in Online Security

Of course, part of the industry's seriousness regarding Internet security is driven by the fact that the federal government—including Congress, the executive branch, bank regulatory agencies, and others—are watching as the ultimate overseers of e-commerce.

In that overseer role, Congress (through new laws) and the administration (through government agencies) could mandate security requirements relating to the Internet. The banking industry in general does not want this to happen, preferring instead to advocate a self-regulatory approach in which the industry develops standards for Internet security.

In her testimony, BITS' CEO Catherine Allen called on Congress to do the following:

- Allow the financial services industry to meet its security commitments. "We are serious, proactive, and strongly committed to self-regulation."

- Look to the regulators to conform to congressional policy favoring a flexible, non-governmental approach to developing technology and security procedures.

- "Work with us collaboratively, as you are today, to develop the kind of informed framework that is necessary to foster the growth of electronic commerce in the kinds of safe, sound, and secure ways that are necessary for the confidence of consumers and the growth of the economy."

The government also has a role in overseeing Internet security because it's a national security issue. According to a 1998 directive signed by President Clinton, "...financial services are among the nation's critical infrastructures that must be protected from intentional acts that would threaten the orderly functioning of the economy." The directive mandates the following:

> "Any interruptions or manipulations of these critical functions must be brief, infrequent, manageable, geographically isolated, and minimally detrimental to the welfare of the United States."

Security Is Not a One-Way Street

Despite the steps that financial services industry players have taken in pursuing and ensuring Internet security, consumers have a responsibility, too. "We would like to emphasize that security is a shared responsibility," Allen told the congressional panel. Consumers, she said, should do the following:

- Become knowledgeable about online banking services. (Hey, you bought this book! Great job!)

- Investigate their online bank to ensure that it is federally insured.

- Actively ask questions of their financial services provider to learn how best to continually protect the security of their transactions.

- Limit unauthorized access to their personal computer.

- Protect their personal identification number (PIN) and passwords.

- Create PINs and passwords that cannot be readily identified.

- Install and regularly update virus detection and eradication software on their personal computers.

- Use a browser that is configured properly and that supports secure and private transactions. (Some online bank sites, such as Wells Fargo's site at *www.wellsfargo.com*, can help you evaluate your Web browser software to ensure that it is up to date with current security and encryption standards.)

- Do not open email attachments from unknown or untrusted sources.

- Do not install pirated software or software from an unknown source.
- When finished using online banking services, log off completely, and then close and restart their browsers before doing other Internet activities.

What You Should Know Now

This chapter addressed the broad issues of security on the Internet and also looked at what banks are doing to educate consumers about security practices. We've also examined the federal government's overseer role in ensuring the integrity of finance and commerce activities on the Internet.

- The Internet is a secure environment, and online financial services providers along with other e-commerce players have every interest in ensuring that this remains so.
- The better online banks do a good job in explaining what security measures are used to protect consumers as well as how they're used. These online banks are working to educate consumers early on with easy-to-recognize buttons or links from their Internet home pages.
- The government's role in Internet security is primarily as an overseer. So far, the government has been fairly hands-off regarding the Internet, allowing e-commerce providers, such as online banks, to develop and implement "best practices" for ensuring the integrity and security of the Internet as a safe place for consumers to do business.
- Although both online banks and the government have vested interests in the security of the Internet and are working to ensure that it remains a safe and secure environment, security is not a one-way street. Consumers (that's us) need to learn about the Internet, e-commerce, and security. Consumers also need to follow certain steps to help ensure Internet security. We'll get into the details of what you can do to guard your security in the next chapter.

CHAPTER 12

The Dark Arts: Cryptography and Encryption

Cryptography and encryption provide the security you need when you access your online bank. In general, common security measures used by online banking providers are of the highest order available or allowed by the federal government.

Remember, *trust* is a bank's middle name (it's often the bank's last name). Many financial institutions have decades of experience ensuring transaction security for their customers in the physical world. This investment of time, energy, and resources is being carried into the virtual world, too.

What You'll Learn in This Chapter:
- How encryption works.
- How you can help ensure security.
- Steps to take if you forget your password.

The Security Debate

Basically, encryption technologies represent locks and keys to data in our information age. These technologies are designed to protect sensitive information transmitted over computer networks. They operate by scrambling and encoding information so that communications can be kept confidential between a sender and recipient.

Cryptography, encryption, and data security is, and will likely remain, a controversial topic.

> **Some Key Definitions**
>
> *Cryptography* describes the field of using codes and encryption to exchange sensitive information between two or more parties.
>
> *Encryption* is the process of using codes or software to scramble a sensitive message so that it is unintelligible to anyone other than the appropriate recipient of the message.
>
> *Data security* refers to procedures and practices used to protect sensitive computer networks and equipment. Both cryptography and encryption are among those procedures and practices.

Law enforcement authorities would like to be able to examine computer files as part of their criminal investigation authorization and would like to see the lower levels of encryption used to ensure Internet security. Consumer and freedom-of-speech advocates argue that such investigative policies intrude on the private lives of law-abiding citizens. They believe consumers should be able to rest assured that all their data being transmitted through the Internet is protected with the best encryption available.

This debate will undoubtedly continue; it is a healthy aspect of the development of the Internet as a place to exchange information and conduct business. The debate also continues with the ongoing dialog regarding individuals' rights and freedoms balanced with law enforcement's efforts that date back to the birth of the United States. Should we be able to transmit our data in systems that not even the government can intercept and read?

What Is Encryption?

In a nutshell, *encryption* means taking a normal message such as "Watson, come here I need you" and converting it into *ciphertext*, which looks and reads like gibberish unless you have the ability to *decrypt* the message.

When it's in ciphertext, our message might look like "adgdbq zncc udkj e wssx arf." (We ran our original, readable message—called *plaintext*—through an Enigma program. This program mimics the Enigma encryption system used by the German military and broken by the Allies in World War II. We go into some detail with Engima encryption later in this chapter.)

THE DARK ARTS: CRYPTOGRAPHY AND ENCRYPTION

Most online banking providers ensure security through Netscape's Secure Sockets Layer protocol (SSL). SSL provides privacy for data transmitted between your Web browser and your online bank's computer, which is often referred to as a *server*.

SSL uses encryption to ensure security and confidentiality. Here's how: When an SSL session is started, your Web browser (such as Netscape Navigator or Microsoft Internet Explorer) sends its public key to your online bank's server so that the bank can securely send a secret key to your browser.

A *public key* is the published portion of an encryption system. It allows for the transmission of a *secret key*, which is known only by the holder of the private, or secret key.

Internet encryption is based on a mathematical algorithm that uses this secret key. The secret key is a binary number that is typically from 40–128 bits in length. As the number of bits in the key increases, the number of possible mathematical key combinations increases, as does the level of security.

In computer terms, a binary number is a number stored in binary form (that is, a number that is represented as a series of 0s and 1s). Within 1 byte (8 bits) of data, the values from 0–255 can be represented. Two bytes of data (16 bits) can store values from 0–65,535.

These value capacities increase exponentially. This is why 128-bit encryption is stronger than 40-bit encryption. With more possible values represented, it would take longer to break a message that uses 128-bit encryption.

More Bits Means More Possible Values:
It takes longer to break a 128-bit encrypted code than a 40-bit code because of the additional number of possible mathematical combinations.

The First Cryptographer

Cryptography, described as the conversion of information into a secret code, has been around for more than 500 years.

Johannes Trithemius (tre TAY me us), a Benedictine monk in Spanheim, Germany, is credited as the first practitioner of cryptography. He wrote *Polygraphiae libri ses* ("Six Books of Polygraphy"), which is viewed by historians as the first published treatise on cryptography.

Trithemius' *Polygraphiae* was published in 1518, two years after his death. In 1499, he wrote *Steganographia* ("Covered Writing"). This manuscript, which was widely circulated, described a cipher, or encryption

continues

continued

> code, in which each letter is represented by words in successive columns of text in a book of prayer.
>
> One portion of Trithemius' *Steganographia,* the once-mysterious third book, has been revealed by cryptanalysts and scholars as written almost completely in code. The third book contains hidden cipher messages within what a casual reader would think is a book about magic, a point that had been debated up until the mid-1990s.
>
> The title of Trithemius' *Steganographia* gives rise to *steganography,* a word used to describe a messaging technique of hiding one type of computer file within another. This technique is sometimes used as an alternative to encryption.

How Banks Use Encryption

Most online banking systems use 128-bit encryption, which is the highest level of encryption allowed by the federal government. The federal government's policy is aimed at terrorists and other criminals. For example, the export of 128-bit encryption is prohibited unless "key recovery" is provided to a third party, such as law enforcement authorities. This allows for the recovery of data but, for obvious reasons, rankles privacy advocates. Information is encrypted mathematically by combining the bits in the key with the data bits. At the receiving end, the secret key is used to unlock the code and restore the original data.

As a result of this secret hand-shaking between your computer and your online bank's computer, data can be exchanged securely and confidentially during your banking session.

Many experts believe it is much safer to put your credit card online than it is to leave it with a waiter or bartender. When you give people your credit card in the offline world, there's a much greater possibility that the carbon copy of the charge slip will be taken out of the garbage and used or that the card number will be simply stolen by your merchant.

The biggest threat to putting your credit card number online is not that it will be intercepted. The real concerns is that the business or bank you are dealing with could have dishonest employees working behind the scenes who might misuse your information.

The SSL security standard for data transfer is expected to be superseded at some point by a new Internet security protocol called Transport Layer Security (TLS). This new standard is backward-compatible with the SSL standard.

A major plus in favor of TLS is that it uses a triple Data Encryption Standard (DES). Simply put, that means that TLS uses three "keys" to encrypt messages. And, when it comes to encryption, more is better than fewer (it's like having three locks on a door rather than one).

Other Security Measures a Bank Can take

Another Internet security measure that online banks typically employ is a firewall. An Internet *firewall* is a physical computer system that enforces a security policy between an organization's network and the Internet.

A firewall determines which inside services can be accessed from the outside over the Internet. On the flip side, a firewall also determines which outside services can be accessed by insiders. In effect, the firewall computer filters attempts to access the bank's main computer where sensitive data resides; it also filters attempts from users at the bank to access the Internet.

For a firewall to work, all traffic to and from the Internet and the bank's main computer must pass through it. The firewall then inspects the traffic and permits only authorized information to pass.

According to the technology company 3Com, an Internet firewall helps organizations, such as online banking providers, define a central "choke point" that keeps unauthorized users, such as hackers, crackers, vandals, and spies, out of a protected network.

Firewall Clarification: Although it's easier to think about a firewall as a separate computer that physically separates the bank's main server from the Internet, the firewall can also be filtering software that resides on the main computer.

> "Firewalls offer a convenient point where Internet security can be monitored and alarms generated," says the company. "It should be noted that for organizations that have connections to the Internet, the question is not whether but *when* attacks will occur."

Shedding Light on the Enigma

One of the keys to the Allied victory in World War II was their code-breaking efforts focused on the German military's Enigma machine.

The Enigma machine randomly encrypted messages and was thought to be unbreakable. It wasn't, thanks to some very smart people, and important German military intelligence thus became available to the Allies on a timely basis. The lesson here is that *any encryption system is breakable*, if those trying to break it are given enough time (years in some cases).

However, simply breaking an encrypted message may not be enough. To illustrate, the Allies' code-breaking of the Enigma machine wouldn't have been very helpful if it took months to understand a single message. Meaningful military strategies could not have been developed had there been such a time lag in message decryption.

Our point here is that being able to decrypt an encrypted message that is months or years old is not of much practical value. In general, with current online banking encryption standards, it would take several years to decrypt a transaction, thus offering an unscrupulous person little or nothing to gain.

A number of experts have developed Internet-based Java applets to demonstrate how the Enigma machine operated. (A *Java applet* is a simple program that operates as part of a Web page.) You can try to encrypt and decrypt a message yourself using one of these applets.

Try It Yourself

1. To find an Enigma applet, go to a search engine such as Google.com (*www.google.com*) and search for the term *Enigma applet*. The search engine should return a list of applets designed to mimic the operation of the Enigma encryption machine.

2. Click one of the hot links for an Enigma applet. You'll have to wait a brief period for the applet to load.

3. You'll then be able to experiment with the Enigma mechanical encryption system (and your school-age children will get extra credit in history).

What's Your Password?

The following are some suggestions we've gleaned for maintaining secure passwords. Do not use any of the following as your password:

- Any variation of your computer login name, full name, birth date, Social Security number, or any other personal information

- Dictionary words, place names, or proper names of any kind or from any language

- Jargon, slang, acronyms, the names of literary characters, movie characters, or celebrities

- Any word or name spelled backwards, with or without interspersed punctuation marks, symbols, or numbers (for example, !n!o!s!i!r!r!a!H is a bad choice for a password)

- Any variation of your name, address, license plate number, telephone number, or other information that can possibly be accessible to others

- Your pets' names or the names of any family members

- The first letters of the words of a common phrase, such as *igwt* for "In God we trust"

Generating a Secure Password

We scouted the Internet in a search for how to best generate a secure password, which you'll need for online banking. We found a good system that randomly generates passwords at *www.diceware.com*.

The Diceware system requires dice. Various rolls of the dice are used to determine a password from a list of words, which can be downloaded from the Diceware site. The password system allows for different password lengths based on what you need.

The Diceware site provides a thorough background on the importance of random password generation, as well as instructions on how to use dice to create secure computer passwords.

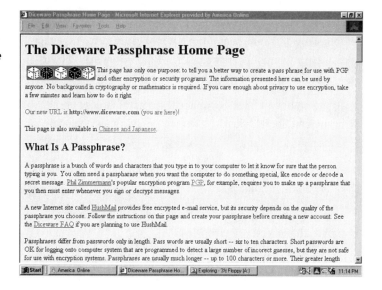

The Diceware system also allows for the use of special characters, such as #, $, or ! to introduce additional variables into a password. This can be an important feature because, as you read in our password security tips, basic dictionary words can be tried sequentially by a computer hacker running a "brute force" password-cracking program.

Brute force password cracking relies on software designed to try different combinations of symbols, numbers, and letters to gain access to a restricted network. This method is by far the most popular way for computer hackers to cause trouble on the Internet.

However, a brute force attack will not work for online banking. Most online banking systems restrict a user to three incorrect password attempts over a given time period, such as a few days or weeks. Then, on the fourth attempt, access to that user's account is automatically shut down.

This should help you sleep better at night.

What do you do if you mess up and are locked out of your online bank? (Don't laugh, this has happened to us.) Call your online bank. A staff member should be able to walk you through what you'll need to do to get up and running (and banking) again.

Security Steps You Can Take

Along with following our password tips, you can take some additional security steps to protect your online banking experience.

For one thing, don't write your password down or allow your browser to store your online banking password on your computer. Doing so could provide the opportunity to anyone with access to your computer to simply turn it on, log on to the Internet, and access your bank accounts online.

Also, we don't recommend that you bookmark your online bank's Web site or list it under Favorites in your Web browser software. This makes possible access to your online bank that much easier.

You're probably thinking that much of our advice here is common sense. Our answer: *It is.* However, it's important to understand and think about how a stranger in your home might be able to access

- Your computer (typically by just turning it on)
- The Internet (by double-clicking your Internet service provider's icon on your computer's desktop)
- Your online financial services provider (perhaps by rummaging through your desk or work area and finding your password)

If you bank online from your office, you have additional concerns, because it is likely that others have access to your computer as well as knowledge of how to shortcut any startup passwords.

The following are some additional steps to keep in mind to protect your security:

- Completely log off and close out of your Web browser software after completing an online banking session. There is a chance that, when visiting another site, information about your earlier banking session can still be accessible and available in your computer's memory.

- Do not leave your browser open to your online banking provider's Web site. Typically, your online bank will log you off after a certain period of inactivity. Even so, don't walk away from your computer to go run errands and leave an online banking page open onscreen.

- Can neighbors or passers-by see you typing on your computer? Or your co-workers? Passwords can sometimes be picked up by the unscrupulous simply through observation or educated guessing.

- Do not leave blank checks, canceled checks, statements, printouts, or other information about your online bank near your computer. Information from these items could be used by a crook to attempt to hack into your account or simply to write checks on your account. Here again, real-world security measures are similar to cyber-security steps. Don't do anything to make a criminal's job easier.

- Never, ever give your password out to anyone. This goes for your online banking password as well as passwords you may use to gain Internet access through your Internet service provider or other Internet sites. No one has any reason to ask you for your password.

> **I've Lost My Password...**
> It happens to everyone. We've drawn a blank at the ATM several times and one of us—we're not saying who, of course—has lost her wallet several times.
> What to do if you forget your password for your online bank? Call your online bank. They will tell you what you should do to get up and running again.

What You Should Know Now

In this chapter, we've reviewed crytopgraphy and encryption. We discussed how you can employ crytopgraphic techniques to generate secure passwords and steps you can take to enhance your security.

Encryption as part of online banking is generally of the highest order permissible by the government—128-bit encryption, to be exact.

You can help ensure security by using randomly generated passwords, jealously guarding passwords, and following other basic, common-sense security practices.

If you forget your online banking password, call your bank. They can help you get up and running again. Never give your password out. Your online bank representative (or anyone else, for that matter) has no reason to ask you for your password.

CHAPTER 13

Privacy Please! How to Protect Your Privacy and Who Else Cares About It

The development of powerful computers that can store and analyze massive amounts of information is your first sign that privacy should be a top concern to you. Businesses are using the new technologies to conduct what they call *customer relationship management*, which simply means analyzing who you are by ciphering through any and all data about you.

This type of information mining helps banks and other retailers decide what to market to you. For example, a computer will take into consideration your basic demographic information and combine that with previous buying habits such as what you eat, what you wear, where you shop, and how much you spend. The fact that you might get more direct marketing calls, emails, or snail mail as a result of this data gathering might not concern you. But what if your bank is selling personal information about you to other businesses? Your bank may be trustworthy, but are the companies to whom your information is being sold also honest? Do they have employees who are unscrupulous enough to take your information and steal your identity? If so, the next thing you know, you could start getting credit card bills from around the world.

All this may seem like one big paranoia trip, but it's the real world as businesses learn how to better harness the immense power of computers.

The issue of privacy should cause all consumers to have some concerns, but for the online bank customer, it has to be a top priority. When you bank online, you are asked to transmit some of

What You'll Learn in This Chapter:
- ▶ The issues and the players in the privacy game.
- ▶ A look at a few privacy policies.
- ▶ Privacy seals are certifications by third parties.

your most personal information over the World Wide Web. Your Social Security number and birth date are needed to conduct almost any business with a financial institution. That's why there is a lot of discussion between the banking industry and the government about what must be done to protect consumers' privacy while banking online.

The federal government has tended to take a *laissez-faire* approach to how business is conducted on the Internet, but a few laws have been passed and banking regulatory agencies are monitoring privacy on the Web closely. This somewhat hands-off approach to privacy and e-commerce has been viewed as a means to encourage rapid innovation and development of the Internet as a vehicle for finance and commerce.

Jodie Bernstein, director of the Federal Trade Commission's Bureau of Consumer Protection, has a lot to say about privacy and e-commerce. When she's online, privacy is a top concern. "I usually ask if they have a privacy policy, and if the answer is 'no,' I'm likely to say 'thank you very much' and go to another site," she says. "What information do you need from me so that I can buy my pantyhose? What are you going to do with that information? I don't want to get a lot of weight loss ads mailed to me."

Who Else Cares About Your Privacy?

Privacy has proven to be a top consumer issue in online banking. Studies show that consumers want the ability to control their information and to be comfortable with how it is used. Banks and the government have taken notice. Both are backing policies and laws that they say will protect the consumer, whether online or off. But frankly, there's a compromise mentality at work. Everyone wants to ensure privacy, but the industry—sometimes with backing from the government—believes that privacy policies also have to recognize that businesses need to exchange certain information to become better marketers and sellers and, therefore, more profitable.

U.S. businesses of all sorts are facing another big privacy issue from beyond our shores: The European Union won't allow its businesses to work with U.S. businesses if they don't adhere to strong privacy standards. Europeans don't really appreciate our government's hands-off approach to online regulation. But the U.S. Commerce Department is attempting to negotiate with the EU a compromise. The gist of the proposal: Give U.S. companies a vote of confidence if they adhere to strong privacy principles, even if the federal government isn't passing laws to enforce these standards.

> **Are You Really Who You Say You Are?**
>
> There's a burgeoning concern about "identity theft" in the online and offline worlds. Thieves are gathering information about you—your address, passwords, Social Security number, telephone numbers, email addresses, medical records, and whatever they can get that helps them pretend they are you. After they gather enough information, for example, they will apply for a credit card and start sending you to the cleaners. The credit card bills are in your name and they are going unpaid. Your credit ratings sink to the bottom of the sea.
>
> How can you avoid becoming a victim of this crime?
>
> Truste, a third-party privacy seal provider, offers these suggestions: don't list your full name in a telephone book; don't put addresses or driver's license numbers on checks; keep your mother's maiden name private; shred financial, medical, and other personal documents before discarding; request security codes for your telephone and bank accounts; give out your Social Security number only in very special circumstances; if you suspect that someone is using your identity, call your local law enforcement agency.

What's the Government Doing to Protect Your Privacy?

President Clinton has outlined a broad proposal to protect financial privacy. His administration wants to limit the sharing of information and require institutions to inform consumers of plans to share or sell their financial data. One of the White House's biggest concerns is the sharing of medical information between financial services providers.

Cross-industry mergers and consolidation are making medical information more accessible to banks. Should a consumer take a physical exam to get an insurance policy, and should the results of that visit be used to lower credit card limits? This scenario seems farfetched but, with the convergence of the insurance, banking, and securities businesses, the sharing of information is getting easier for corporations and scarier for consumers.

When the president announced his plan to enhance financial services privacy, he said, "You should not have to worry that the result of your latest physical exam will be used to deny you a home mortgage or a credit card." When Congress passed its financial services modernization law in 1999, it addressed some of the president's concerns, but not all. In fact, some consumer advocates feel the new law was a setback to consumer privacy. The reality: It represents a Washington compromise where both sides gained and lost a little ground.

What does the new banking law do on the privacy front? The law does the following:

- Prohibits banks and all financial institutions from disclosing customer account numbers or access codes to unaffiliated third parties for telemarketing or direct marketing purposes.

- Enables consumers to opt out of having their personal financial information shared with unaffiliated third parties in almost all cases, except if the bank shares information with an unaffiliated third party that performs functions for the bank. An example of an unaffiliated third party is a company, such as an insurance provider, that is not under a bank's corporate umbrella. In such an instance, although the bank doesn't have to give the consumer the right to opt out, the bank does have to fully disclose the information-sharing to the consumer and require the third party to maintain confidentiality of the information.

- Requires that banks annually disclose their privacy policies to customers. Although many online banks do this now, this is no longer a *suggestion* from the government but a *requirement*.

- Prohibits persons from misrepresenting themselves to obtain personal information about others (this seems like a no-brainer). This part of the law is directed at identity pirates who are in the business of gathering as much personal information about consumers as they can and then selling it.

A *New York Times* report on the new law included a great quote from David Komansky, the head of Merrill Lynch, showing the delicate balance of consumer and industry concerns in the privacy debate. The story quoted Komansky reflecting on the impact of the law: "I have two points of view. As an individual and consumer, I think that I am entitled to certain privacies. The things that concern me are health records as they apply to mortgages applications, for example—I want to have those protections… As a business person, having the option to data-mine investment traits of clients can position us to be able to more efficiently market our products. It's an important advantage and something I value."

> **A Medium-Rare Deal**
>
> The consumer could have gotten a much better deal with the new law. For example, we are given an opportunity to opt-out of having the bank share information with unaffiliated third parties. This, in essence, puts the burden on us, the customer. The legislators could have made this provision more consumer-friendly by saying banks must give us the option of opting *in*. That would have meant that our information would be shared only if we gave permission. That wouldn't have put the burden of privacy on us!
>
> On the positive side for consumers, the new law makes it clear that banks have to at least send their privacy policies to consumers. In the online world, those policies are usually posted on the home page.

The new law is important to online banking because of the enhanced power that electronic commerce gives to financial institutions. With the new capabilities allowed by faster and smarter computers, banks are collecting more data on their customers than ever before.

Hence, banking regulators have a few specific policies for the online banking world. The Federal Deposit Insurance Corporation and the Office of Thrift Supervision have both advised banks that they regulate to post *privacy seals* and to provide consumers a chance to opt out of a plan to collect information for marketing purposes. Banks have also been advised to notify consumers about how information will be used and to allow access to collected information so consumers can see whether it is accurate.

> **Privacy Seals**
>
> Don't get confused between a privacy policy and a privacy seal. Here are their simple definitions.
>
> An online *privacy policy* is a statement by a bank or any e-commerce business indicating to you how it will use the information it gathers about you as you surf its site. Policies will tell you, for example, that the business is asking you for your address so that it can mail to you marketing materials.
>
> An online *privacy seal* is a completely different story. A seal is granted to a bank or business by an organization that suggests and monitors whether the institution is adhering to certain privacy guidelines. A seal tells a consumer that a third party is making sure that the bank follows certain privacy rules. Banks usually have to pay the third party to investigate them and get the seal.

What Are Banks Doing to Protect Your Privacy?

To avoid too much government oversight, the banking industry has banded together to try to police itself. This coming together has resulted in privacy and security certification seals and the issuance of principles by industry associations. The BBBOnline privacy seal, for example, shows that the bank has allowed the Better Business Bureau to review its privacy policies for effectiveness.

BBBOnline charges a bank to participate in this online privacy program. Under the agreement between the bank and BBBOnline, the institution must adhere to BBBOnline's guidelines or they lose permission to display the seal on its site. For example, the guidelines include that the certified online business must explain to consumers what is being collected and why. BBBOnline also insists that the business agree to random audits of its system and to participate in dispute resolution procedures if a consumer has a complaint.

Why would a bank want to pay BBBOnline for this service? Because the customer will more likely trust the bank or any e-commerce site if it displays the trusted symbol of the Better

Business Bureau. In the online world, the seals are usually listed at the bottom of the home page.

Although these seals are popular in the e-commerce world at large, they have not been widely adopted among banks as of yet. As a lt, you won't see too many of them at online bank sites. Banks believe they don't need the seals because their relationship with customers is based on trust.

Banking trade associations, however, have drafted the U.S. Banking Industry Privacy Principles, the Banking Industry Technology Secretariat has created a Privacy Principles Implementation Plan, and other industry executives have formed the Online Privacy Alliance at *www.privacyalliance.org*. This latter group represents companies trying to enforce privacy guidelines on one another. The American Institute of Certified Public Accountants has also launched a privacy assurance program.

What Does a Privacy Policy Look Like and Where Can I Find One?

Privacy policies vary widely, but most start with the language, "We recognize the importance of protecting your personal information." From there, policies vary greatly. You also never know exactly where a privacy policy will appear on a Web site. Sometimes it's on the first page, and sometimes it's buried and almost impossible to find. This section discusses what some of the major e-banks are doing on privacy.

Security First Network Bank (*www.sfnb.com*) posts its privacy policy front-and-center, as you can see in the following figure; you can't miss it. The link to the privacy policy is at the top of the home page. This is not always the case; many times the links to the policy are on the side, at the bottom of the first page, or placed deep into the site where no reasonable person can find it. You go, SFNB!

The Security First Network Bank makes the link to a privacy policy a top priority on their Web page. Click Your Privacy to read what SFNB will do to protect you.

The language of the SFNB site is not remarkable, but it's clear. It tells you when the institution collects personal information, how the information is used, and it proclaims, "Does Security First Network Bank provide information to external parties? Absolutely not!" But the bank clarifies this statement by saying that it will share information with a company that is helping it carry out its business. For example, it will share information with the company managing its ATM and debit cards.

We're Watching You:

Yikes! Privacy is a top concern for consumers online. In a survey by Privacy and American Business, a whopping 81 percent of Internet users and 79 percent of Internet consumers were concerned about threats to their privacy online.

On the other hand, the First Internet Bank of Indiana (*www.firstib.com*) doesn't display its privacy policy on the first page. In fact, the link to the policy is hard to find. After clicking through the site, we found it on a page titled "About First IB." Its policy looks like that of many other online banks, but a close read shows just how far an institution will go to collect information about you.

First, IB collects a lot of details about you while you are on its site. While you are just surfing around, the bank is, in essence, reading over your shoulder. The privacy policy explains just how much it might learn: "First IB is committed to continuous improvement of our Web site. We may use software tools to gather information about site visitors' browsing activities in order to target areas for improvement. Information gathered may include date and time of visits, pages viewed, time spent at the site, browser types, Internet service provider, and the site visited just before and just after the First IB site." That's a lot of information, but at least the bank tells you what it's doing.

Wingspan Bank (*www.wingspan.com*) places its privacy policy at the bottom of its first Web page. It's one of the more detailed policies online. It also allows consumers opening a checking or credit card account, obtaining an unsecured installment loan, or buying a certificate of deposit the option of providing necessary information by telephone or mail instead of by transmitting it online.

CompuBank (*www.compubank.com*) has its privacy policy hidden on its security page. Although security and privacy are separate issues, there is enough overlap that you can understand this juxtaposition. Still, the policy is hard to find when you first get to the site, shown in the following figure.

CompuBank puts its privacy policy on a security page, which may not be an obvious connection to a customer visiting the Web site.

CompuBank has three seals at the bottom of its page to give the consumer more confidence about its privacy and security: BBBOnline, TravelersProperty Casualty, and VeriSign. You can click each seal to learn more about what they mean. Like other banks, one part of CompuBank's privacy policy is very helpful to the consumer: The bank provides an email address and phone number that customers can use to check what information has been gathered about them.

What's Behind Those Seals?

Bankers view the online world as the wild, wild West. It's their new frontier, promising expanded markets and more efficient ways to serve customers. But just as many a sheriff wasn't much liked in the days when our country was rushing west to find gold, banks aren't exactly hankering for government oversight of cyberspace. To prevent the government from passing too many laws, banking and other industries are attempting to police themselves.

BBBOnline is the Better Business Bureau's attempt to bring its mission to the online world. BBBOnline has three seal programs, one for reliability, one for general privacy, and one for children's privacy. Companies that display the reliability seal have agreed to fair advertising standards, established by the Better Business Bureau, to respond promptly to consumer complaints and to commit to independent third-party dispute resolution.

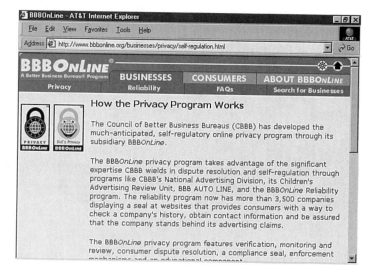

BBBOnline is betting that its good name will bring consumer confidence to online commerce. That BBB image has a long history in the offline world.

Truste is a nonprofit privacy initiative. It provides third-party oversight of the privacy standards at sites. Companies join the initiative, have their systems certified, and then carry the Truste seal, usually found at the bottom of the first page of the Web site. Similar to that of BBBOnline, the intention of this initiative is to increase the confidence of consumers when they are conducting e-commerce.

PRIVACY PLEASE! HOW TO PROTECT YOUR PRIVACY AND WHO

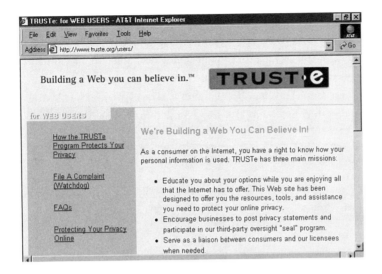

This seal from Truste is all about privacy, indicating that the site has taken steps to protect your personal information. Truste has a good reputation with online watchdogs.

VeriSign does more than certify sites as secure. It also sells a security infrastructure to the banks, meaning that it provides advice and computer technology to ensure security. The company has partnered with some of the larger players on the Internet, including Visa, Netscape, Microsoft, and America Online.

When you see this VeriSign check mark, you can be assured that the Web site has taken an extra step to secure your information.

TravelersProperty Casualty is unlike other seals that certify whether a system is secure or maintains privacy standards.

Instead, this seal is displayed on the sites of online banks that provide their customers with insurance protection against unauthorized transactions from their online accounts. This insurance protection is provided by a SafeWeb Remote Banking Insurance policy from Travelers Bond, a unit of TravelersProperty Casualty. The policy insures you for up to $4,000 in losses.

Who doesn't feel safe under the familiar Travelers red umbrella?

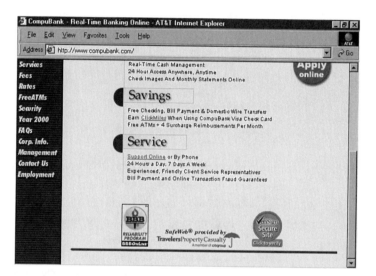

The Gold Standard for a Bank's Privacy Policy

Government regulators haven't yet mandated what should go into a privacy policy. They are only making strong suggestions. The following are the suggested elements that should appear in privacy statements. If a policy has these components, you know the bank is at least trying to be consumer friendly. These principles have been developed by the Federal Trade Commission.

- A notice to consumers about information-gathering practices before any personal information is collected

- Choice for consumers about the collection and use of information from or about them and the option to restrict use of the information

- Security and accuracy of consumer information collected protecting against loss, unauthorized access, and disclosure of information

- Access for consumers to information collected and the ability to identify and correct errors in a timely and inexpensive manner

- Enforcement and consumer redress to ensure compliance with the privacy policy and information practices and a means of recourse for an injured party

What You Should Know Now

Privacy is a top concern of most Internet users; you shouldn't be any different. Always read your bank's privacy statements. That's where you can learn what it intends to do with the information it collects about you.

The government has a laissez-faire attitude about placing mandates on the e-commerce world. You have to be the one who protects your own privacy.

Look for privacy seals on your bank's Web site. These seals can help you have peace of mind that the bank's privacy policies are being monitored by a third party.

CHAPTER 14

Your Privacy and Security Checklist

Privacy and security are two of the hottest issues in the online banking world. If we, as consumers, don't feel as though our money is safe and our information is private, we just won't use an online service. And that's not good for banks.

In the two previous chapters, we gave you the details about the security and privacy policies at banks. In this chapter, we want to give you the best tips to help you proactively protect your money and identity when online banking.

10 Privacy Consumer Tips

The following words of caution on how to protect your privacy are good advice for you when banking online—and when you are conducting *any* e-commerce:

- *Look for posted privacy policies*—It's a great way to learn directly why a bank is asking for certain information. Regulators aren't *mandating* that privacy policies be posted as of this writing, but they are *advising* that policies be posted on sites. If your bank doesn't have a policy at its site, call and ask why. If it refuses to give you the policy, choose another bank.

- *Don't give out personal information if it isn't necessary for the particular transaction*—For example, why should you tell a bank your mother's birth date when you are opening a checking account? The institution might want that information to market flowers to you on that day, but providing that information isn't vital to the opening of the account. Call the bank and ask why this information is being collected.

What You'll Learn in This Chapter:
- ▶ The bottom line on protecting your privacy.
- ▶ Aggressive security steps you can take.
- ▶ How online banks are trying to outmaneuver hackers.

- *Know that certain information is more sensitive than other data*—Your birth date, Social Security number, and mother's maiden name should only be given when you feel comfortable that the information will be used properly. Why your mother's maiden name? The banking industry has determined that the chance of any stranger knowing that about you is very remote. Because of that, the industry has adopted that information as one of the secret codes to have access to information about your accounts.

- *Parts of your bank's site are secure, and others aren't*—If you are emailing the bank from its site, ask first whether its email is secure. If not, don't email the bank information from there. Most email is *not* secure and, therefore, is not private.

- *Never give out your passwords*—Passwords have become as sacred as our mothers. There are a few bank sites that have begun asking you to share passwords of your accounts with other companies. If you do share your password, you will have access to balances at one site, in one glance, for accounts you may have with any number of businesses (including airline frequent flyer programs or grocery store purchasing points). If your bank offers this capability, you should call and achieve a comfort level with the security of the system before giving it your passwords.

- *If asked for a credit card number, make sure that your system and that of the bank's is secure*—If someone steals your credit card number, you will only be responsible for $50, but it can wreak havoc with your credit ratings, which can take a long time to fix.

- *If you are the type who needs third-party confirmation about serious matters such as privacy, look to see if your bank's policy is certified by other organizations*—Some of the seals to look for are BBBOnline, Truste, and VeriSign.

- *Beware of scam sites*—Never give personal information to a site that you aren't 100 percent sure is legitimate. If you decide to do business with an online bank, make sure it's legitimate. Go to the FDIC site at *www.fdic.gov* and click the *Is My Bank Insured?* link. It's a great way to verify your bank's trustworthiness.

- *See whether you can stop cookies*—If you don't like cookies—those files sent to your computer by Web sites to track your online activities—you may be able to stop them. Some browsers can stop cookies and others can warn you when you are about to get one deposited on your hard drive.

- *Look for alternative methods of providing information*—If you are uncomfortable for any reason with giving your bank information online, call your bank and ask whether you can provide the information over the phone or with snail mail. Some banks list these options in their privacy policies.

10 Security Consumer Tips

Banks are doing a lot with technology to ensure the security of their systems. But you can help ensure security with a little common sense.

- *Security starts at your desktop*—When banking online, the security of your transactions isn't only up to the bank. It's also up to you. Never log on to your online bank's site and just walk away from your computer, especially if you're banking on a computer in a workplace or some other location where others have access to your system. Some bank sites realize, however, just how forgetful some of us can be. Many of the online banks will automatically log you off if your screen is left idle. This policy is for your own good. If your bank doesn't do this already, ask it to add this safety function.

- *Make sure that your bank is federally insured*—This is easy to do, and besides, you'll feel like a sleuth in the process. Log on to the Federal Deposit Insurance Corporation's Web site at *www.fdic.gov*. On the left bar, click the *Is My Bank Insured?* box; you will soon find out whether your institution of choice is a bank backed by the full faith and credit of the

U.S. government. If your bank doesn't show up in the FDIC database, call (800) 934-FDIC or email *consumer@fdic.gov* to ask why. There are some banks licensed to do business that aren't members of the FDIC. However, the standard in the industry is definitely to be a member and to offer consumers the assurances of federal deposit insurance.

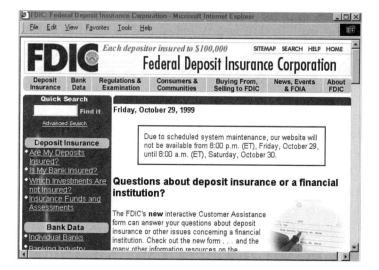

When you check at consumer@fdic.gov, *this is what the screen will look like if your bank is a member of the FDIC.*

- *Make sure that your bank exists*—Some companies that aren't banks use the word *bank* in their names. The government has already shut down two sites that weren't banks but were using the names Freedom Bank and Netware International Bank. As noted in the preceding tip, check with the FDIC, call your state banking department or any of the federal regulators to verify the legitimacy of the institution. One sure sign that something might not be right is rates that are too good to be true. If you think a site is suspicious, report it to the FDIC. The FDIC gives details on how to make suspicious bank reports at *www.fdic.gov/bank/individual/online/sspcious.html.*

- *After using online banking services, log off before going to other Internet sites*—To be extra careful, close your browser when you're done with your banking activities and restart it when you continue other online activities. Some sites like to track where you've been just before you visit and just after. You can prevent this snooping by just logging off.

- *Use only a secure browser that supports private transactions*—The browsers accepted by most online banks are Netscape Navigator, Netscape Communicator, and Microsoft Internet Explorer. Many bank sites will allow you to download a secure browser if your system doesn't already have one. Some banks will let you check your browser at its site. If you don't know what browser you have, you do a simple check at the Wells Fargo site (*http://wellsfargo.com/per/services/security/security2/*) to find out.

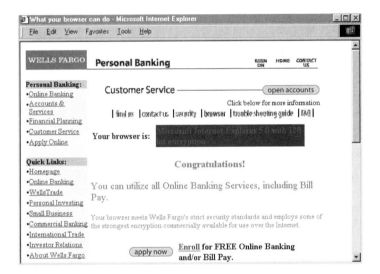

The first page of the Wells Fargo site has a Security Guarantee button. Click it. When you get to the Customer Service page, click Test Your Browser. If your browser is online banking ready, you'll see a screen like this one.

- *Protect your computer from viruses*—This is a constant process. There are always new viruses. You must buy virus-protection software and upgrade it (that service is free) on a regular basis. Some bank sites, like Wells Fargo, will let you buy this software online at its site.

- *Be very wary of doing business with foreign banks*—Many foreign banks aren't FDIC insured. If the bank closes, you won't get your money back. One foreign bank on the Internet that closed was the European Union Bank based in the West Indies.

- *Know where to get help*—In addition to the government regulators, know that you can get help from your state attorney general's office. Also, if you feel that you were victimized by fraud, contact the Internet Fraud Watch of the National Fraud Internet Center at *www.fraud.org*. The center will forward reports to the appropriate government agency.

- *Get a referral*—The industry might disagree with this tip, but before you sign on with a bank, try to find another person who already is a customer. Another consumer can serve as your best source for knowing whether there are any major security problems with the bank.

- *Adhere to basic Internet safety tips*—The long list of basic Internet safety tips also apply to online banking, including limiting access to your computer, protecting your PIN and passwords, creatively creating your passwords, refraining from opening email attachments from unknown sources, and refraining from installing pirated software.

Just How Much Does Industry Care About Security? A Lot

One of the basic operating principles of your bank is trust. A bank knows it wouldn't have your business unless you trust it with your money. Maintaining this trustworthiness is key to a bank's success.

That's why some of the biggest players in the industry have created the BITS Financial Services Security Laboratory. Banks backing this project include the giants First Union Corp., Bank of America, BankBoston, Bank One, Chase Manhattan, Citigroup, and Wells Fargo.

The BITS testing lab, based in Reston, Virginia, is where online banking security systems are tested and developed to stay ahead of the efforts of hackers. Cybercriminals are always trying to break into banking systems, but they have had very little success so far. One reason is because businesses as a whole are always looking for ways to stay one click ahead of the bad guys.

The technicians in the BITS lab have created a seal to certify testing of security-related technology. The lab also has created an information-sharing and analysis center to alert the industry to new security threats.

Companies that make the software and design the electronic systems for online banks bring their products to the BITS lab to be tested by in-house hacking experts. If a bank's system proves immune to attacks by the BITS hackers, the system is awarded a certification seal from the lab. This seal helps banks know before they buy into these online banking systems just how secure the systems are.

YOUR PRIVACY AND SECURITY CHECKLIST

What You Should Know Now

Privacy and security are top concerns for you and your bank. But you can take aggressive moves to protect your money and identity over the Internet.

- First things first. Always learn whether the site is a legitimate bank. We've suggested that you find another customer who has banked at the site and ask that person about the bank or check with the FDIC Online (*www.fdic.gov*) to see whether the institution is insured.

- After you know it's a legitimate bank site, practice safe e-banking, get a secure browser, protect your password, and use common sense.

- You can't take too many precautions.

PART IV
The Banking Revolution Is Just Beginning

CHAPTER 15

What Customers Like Best About Their Online Banks

The rule of thumb on the Web: If your page takes longer than 10 seconds to appear on your customers' computers, you've probably already lost them. In the banking world, consumers want a quick visual response to their mouse clicks, and they want transfers from one account to another to take place in real-time.

What You'll Learn in This Chapter:
- The hottest features and functions of online banking.
- Award-winning online banking sites.

> **Speed Comparisons**
>
> If speed on the Internet is your ultimate point of contention, and you want find an online bank that downloads quickly, you can see comparisons at the Gomez Advisors site at *www.gomez.com*. When you've opened the Gomez site, scroll down and check out the How Are the Banks Performing? area. Type the name of the bank you want to check out and *bingo!* You'll see how your bank rates in the industry.

If you make a transfer from your checking account to your savings account on your home computer on a Sunday night, can you rush out to the closest ATM and see that the transfer actually took place? Some bank sites give you this real-time speed; others have systems that are too clumsy or too inefficient to provide that level of responsiveness. It costs a bank about $12,000 to build a Web site that has limited bells and whistles and as much as $500,000 to develop an online, fully-transactional banking site at which you can do all your business in real-time.

Online banking sites compete against one another in all sorts of categories, including what they offer and what they charge you for their services. The industry is still young, so it's taking some banks longer than others to adopt the best features on their domains. In this chapter, we'll tell you what you can expect from the best sites and just which banks keep rating high in online banking beauty contests when compared with other banks.

The Features You Should Expect from the Best

If your bank doesn't have most of these features, we suggest that you shop around. There are many star bank sites out there, and if you use one that doesn't offer the best bells and whistles, you will likely get discouraged and go back to banking offline.

- *Solid security systems*—As discussed in Part III, "The Facts About Security and Privacy," your online bank site should give you details about its security system. If the bank doesn't, this site is probably not where you should be doing business. If you can't find a security statement, call the bank and ask if it has one posted on its site. One special note here: You want the bank to have a system that automatically logs off if it remains idle for a certain amount of time. That's the best way to stamp out fraud on your end if you get called away from your computer by someone at the door or by a barking dog. It's also important to ask your banker whether the institution considers security a one-time accomplishment or an ongoing challenge. Hackers are smart enough these days that your bank needs to think of security upgrading and vigilance as a never-ending task.

    Wells Fargo gives a detailed explanation of its security system. It also gives its online site users a 100 percent guarantee for any funds improperly removed from your account. Check out *http://wellsfargo.com/per/services/security/distributed/*.

Wells Fargo shows how security is important at your PC, over the Internet, and in the bank's own systems. On this page, the bank allows you to click through explanations of how security is maintained at all three locations.

- *Posted privacy policies*—The government doesn't mandate privacy policies yet, but banking regulators have suggested that all bank sites post policies explaining why they take certain information from you, how they will use that information, who they will share it with, give you an opportunity to correct any information they gather about you, and give you a chance to opt-out of any plans to share your personal information with any other business. These policies are often posted at the bottom of the first page of a bank's site. Yes, look for the small print, because it's usually there and is important for you to know.

- *Real-time, not batch processing*—To put up a real-time site, banks have to spend thousands of dollars more on their online operation. But, because consumers are demanding this feature, some banks are making this investment. What's the difference between real-time and batch processing? In a real-time system, transactions are actually made to your account right when you click your mouse. If you transfer $1,000 from your savings account into your checking account, you should be able to see that transaction at an ATM instantly. A *batch processing* system, on the other hand, notes your order to transfer funds; the bank actually makes the transfer after-hours or later in the day. When deciding on a site, just ask a bank representative whether the system is real-time or batch. That's the best way to learn this handy information before you sign on with any bank.

- *The site offers you the world in financial services*—Some sites are somewhat useless. They function simply as electronic brochures. You can learn what a bank has to offer, but you can't do any actual business online. The sites where you can actually do business—*transactional sites*—are what you need for Internet banking. In addition to being transactional, the sites that get the best reviews are those that allow you to do basic banking functions and obtain other financial products, including securities and insurance.

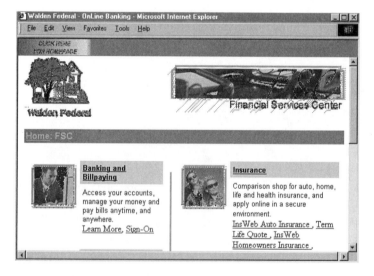

Walden Federal (waldenbank.com) offers its customers a financial services center. Here you have a clear menu of services, from bill paying to investing to shopping.

- *The service is free! Or almost*—How much you get charged for online banking can get complicated. But some policies are simple.

Wingspan has no charge for its checking account, which also earns interest and has no cost for reviewing accounts and transferring funds. Its bill-paying service is also free for 10 payments a month (25 cents for each additional payment) if you have a checking account. If you don't have a checking account, you pay $4.95 per transaction.

Wells Fargo doesn't charge anything for reviewing accounts and transferring funds, but it does charge $5 a month for bill payment, which allows you to pay 25 bills. Any additional bills in a month cost 40 cents apiece.

At Citibank, the online connection is free if you have a regular checking account, and you can pay as many bills as you want at no charge. If you customarily pay bills with a check in the mail, this service could mean a lot in postage stamp savings.

What's odd about all of this is that it is not clear what banks charge for what services. You will have to shop around. It's hard to find any pricing on the actual sites, and only a few will list their fees.

- *You get rebates for ATM fees*—This is becoming an offering by many Internet-only banks. Because they don't have branches or their own ATMs, some Internet banks will reimburse you for any fees a foreign ATM charges your account to get your business. (A *foreign ATM* is any ATM not owned by your bank.)

  Wingspan Bank (*www.wingspan.com*) promotes its ATM rebates on its first page, but you have to click deep into the site to the page that explains the terms of its checking account. There you find that the bank will rebate up to $5 every month. As another example, Compubank (*www.compubank.com*) will give you four $1.50 reimbursements each month.

  Remember:
  Not all rebate policies are alike, and some are hard to find!

- *Bill payment*—The best banks will pay those you owe either electronically or by cutting an actual check. As noted previously, there are different types of payment streams. In all the systems, you may lose the "float" that customarily came when paying bills through the mail. For example, when paying through the mail, you can send your landlord a check on the 25th of the month and your account holds on to those funds until the landlord cashes the check and his or her bank processes it. The time between the day you write the check and the day it is actually cashed is the *float period*. With online banking bill payments, the money is taken out of your account on the same day the bank makes the payment, whether the payment is made by cutting a check or taking out the funds electronically.

- *Twenty-four-hour phone access*—It feels like a treasure hunt sometimes, but the best sites have phone numbers clearly posted. These dream sites also have these lines staffed, 24 hours a day, seven days a week. If your bank only lets you talk to a machine, you aren't getting the best customer service.

Salem Five Cents Savings Bank, based in Salem, Massachusetts, has been a long-time award-winning site. It now has an electronic division (*www.directbanking.com*) from which its customers bank online.

Salem Five Cents has an excellent contact information page. From the bank's home page, the contact information is easy to find, and you have lots of options.

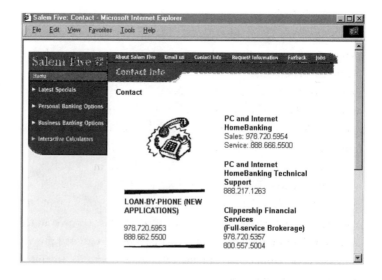

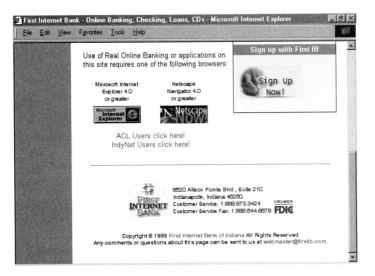

First Internet Bank of Indiana at www.firstib.com makes it easy for its customers. The contact information link is exactly where it should be—on the first page of the site.

And the Winners Are...

The award for "best online bank" is not an Emmy or an Oscar, but online banks are nonetheless fighting for customers and good ratings. Several different companies rate the banks, but the two that stand out and that are quoted most often are a survey by *SmartMoney* and an extensive rating by Gomez Advisors Inc., a company that advises consumers about e-commerce and gives advice to companies on how to be effective online.

In the last survey by *SmartMoney*, which is owned by Dow Jones, the magazine considered 13 of the largest banks and the six Internet-only banks that were up and doing business at the time of its survey. The survey took into consideration six categories: security, fees, level of service, account information, products, and customer service. The last big winner in *SmartMoney*'s survey was CompuBank (*www.compubank.com*), established in 1998 and based in Houston. The magazine proclaimed that this Internet-only bank "...placed first in our survey thanks to nonexistent fees, a smorgasbord of services, and a cutting-edge Web site." In last place was Mellon Bank (*www.mellonbank.com*) for offering "...few online products, a limited Web site, and fees for routine services like the return of cleared checks."

If you visit the CompuBank home page, notice that this institution places its pricing policy front and center. It's easy to see why—its services are free and it offers four ATM surcharge reimbursements each month. Other consumer-friendly features include the click box for 24-hour phone service and a host of security seals.

A quick review of CompuBank's home page shows that this bank clearly understands what's good for consumers.

Gomez Advisors only ranks online banking sites for institutions with $2 billion or more in deposits. The firm uses more than 100 criteria, including whether these online banks guarantee bill payments, provide real-time transactions, and offer customers complete loan applications at the site. In the last ranking by Gomez, the winning bank was Security First Network Bank (*www.sfnb.com*), established in 1998 and based in Atlanta. In hailing this bank, Gomez said, "SFNB holds on to the top spot by offering a tightly integrated suite of deposit and credit card products with online applications, lifetime account histories, and competitive pricing." Another big plus with SFNB is that it maintains a customer phone service 24 hours a day, every day.

Security First Network Bank has a simple-looking home page that is packed with features that make Internet banking easier for the consumer. This page is a winner because it makes access to what you really want very convenient.

At the SFNB site, you can find the guarantees, locate the privacy policy, and access your account very easily. Note also that the contact information is right there on the first page. This bank has nothing to hide.

Gomez Advisors' Top 10 Internet Banks, Fall 1999

You don't have to read *Smart Money* or go to the Gomez site to learn which banks are ranked high in these contests. When the banks are highly ranked, they will make that fact known when you get to their Internet sites. Security First Network Bank (*www.sfnb.com*) proclaims on its first page: "We're number 1, Winter 98, Spring 99, Summer 99, Fall 99 and we're celebrating!" You can click a Gomez seal to see the top five banks for each of those ranking lists.

1. Security First Network Bank, *www.sfnb.com*
2. Wells Fargo, *www.wellsfargo.com*
3. Net.B@nk, *www.netbank.com*
4. First Internet Bank of Indiana, *www.firstib.com*
5. WingspanBank.com, *wingspanbank.com*
6. CompuBank, *compubank.com*
7. Bank One, *www.bankone.com*
8. Citibank, *www.citibank.com*
9. US Access Bank, *usaccessbank.com*
10. Huntington, *www.huntington.com*

Online and Old-Fashioned Banks:

There's a good mix of Internet-only institutions and the old brick and mortar banks in this list. Security First, which ranks number 1, brags in its marketing language that it's "the world's first fully-transactional Internet bank." Ranked just below it is one of our nation's oldest offline world banks, Wells Fargo. We think you can find good service with both types of banks. In reality, they are all starting to look alike as competition intensifies.

> **SmartMoney's Top 10 Internet Banks, June 1999**
> 1. Compubank, *www.compubank.com*
> 2. Citibank, *www.citibank.com*
> 3. Wells Fargo, *www.wellsfargo.com*
> 4. Security First Network, *www.sfnb.com*
> 5. Crestar, *www.crestar.com*
> 6. Net.B@nk, *www.netbank.com*
> 7. Key Bank, *www.key.com*
> 8. USAccess, *www.usaaccessbank.com*
> 9. Wachovia, *www.wachovia.com*
> 10. Bank of America, *www.bankamerica.com*
> 11. Telebank, *www.telebank.com*

What You Should Know Now

Test drive a lot of Internet banking sites and shop around for the good fees and rates. We think the top features to look for when choosing a site are solid security, privacy guarantees, and policy statements. And yes, these features must be easy to find.

It doesn't hurt to see how the experts at *Smart Money* and Gomez Advisors rank online bank sites. Look for the institutions that appear in both lists—such as Compubank, a pure-player, and Citibank, a brick-and-mortar bank with an Internet presence—and compare them by checking out their demos.

CHAPTER 16

The Bottom Line on Sanity and Banking Online

There's fear hovering in the board rooms of banks around the country. Bank directors know that competition lurks just about everywhere. Businesses that traditionally haven't offered banking services are now marketing them along with credit cards, mutual funds, insurance policies, and loans. And just about every type of enterprise online is breaking into the financial services world, whether the company sells clothes, books, or Internet access.

For you, the consumer, this intense competition means that you can demand a little more from whomever you are entrusting with your money. You can and you should.

We think it's good for consumers to remember this power they have with their banks. In many ways, banks have the upper hand, but we think you should just go to another institution if you aren't treated fairly—in either the online or offline world.

Up until this chapter, we hope that we've made banking online seem easy. We aren't going to completely change gears now, but we know that even the most determined consumer will run into trouble now and then. That's why we want to show you a few powerful tools to keep in mind as you venture out with millions of others into the world of banking on the Internet.

Why Consumers Have the Power

When we were growing up, most families didn't have a tough decision when picking a bank: It was usually the bank around the

What You'll Learn in This Chapter:
- That the competition is fierce; it's a consumer's market.
- All about the "clicks" of the trade.
- What to do if you feel you've been burned.

Why Banks Like the Internet:
ebank.com (*www.ebank.com*) says that the average payment transaction over the telephone costs 54 cents; over the Internet, the transaction costs 4 cents; at a bank branch, the cost is $1.44.

corner. Today, your "bank" can be a credit card company, a department store, an investment firm, a traditional bank, or a credit union. And it's rarely located just around the corner.

Many of us are choosing to manage our money with entities called *non-banks*. We are taking our money out of traditional savings and checking accounts. Banks no longer hold the majority of America's wealth. More of us are betting on other money management strategies, including investing in the stock market. For the community bank or credit union, even more competitive factors have been put into play. Internet banks are offering highly competitive rates and marketing their products directly into our living rooms over our home computers. And megabanks are growing into one-stop financial shops as they merge and acquire insurance companies and investing firms.

> **Banks Are Losing Business**
>
> Banks are losing it, literally. From 1990 to 1998, bank shares of private domestic assets fell from 21 percent to 9.2 percent; equities rose from 20.6 percent to 32.8 percent; pensions declined from 20.3 percent to 18.5 percent; mutual funds rose from 3.5 percent to 7.7 percent; and money markets went slightly down from 2.9 percent to 2.8 percent. Banks hope that by getting online and offering a wide variety of products and services, they will regain some of their share of the wealth.
>
> No one is predicting the complete demise of the traditional bank. But the bankers who run these old-fashioned institutions have to wake up and smell the new e-conomy if they are going to survive and thrive in this new century. That includes getting up to speed with the Internet and adding other services, such as small business lending.

Who Wants Your Banking Business?

Who are the newcomers coming after your money? When you're surfing on the Internet or walking down a city street, banking services are now available at many non-traditional locations.

Bill Payment Agencies

In an earlier chapter, we told you how banks want to help you pay your bills. Traditional banks want to provide this service—and so do a host of non-banks on the Internet. *PayMyBills.com* is one of these new competitors.

PayMyBills.com will send you bills through email and allow you to pay them through its Internet system. Here's the way this works: You tell your payees to mail your bills to the PayMyBills address, and PayMyBills then emails the bills to you. When you get the email about the bill, you go to the PayMyBills Internet site and initiate payments. One big plus about this site is that when you move, you never have to worry about whether your bills will find you. If you use this service, your permanent billing address can always be PayMyBills.

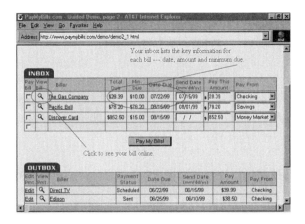

If you use the PayMyBills service, you can have all your bills directed to the company, which will then email you when it receives a bill. You can then go the site at www.paymybills.com and initiate payments.

World Wide Web Be-Alls

One of the Internet giants getting into banking services is *MSN.com*, Microsoft's online ramp on to the World Wide Web. When you open this home page (*www.msn.com*), click the Money button to enter MoneyCentral, Microsoft's comprehensive report on everything you need to know to manage your finances. MoneyCentral has a lot of information about banking and bills, taxes, savings, retirement, and wills.

When we went to the site, we learned a lot about how banks make or lose money off their customers. Did you know that if a bank doesn't generate any fees by giving you a checking account, it loses about $100 a year? On the other hand, the average checking account brings in $200 to $600 in cross-selling profits a year.

MoneyCentral is just another competitive force for banks to reckon with as they go after managing and holding your wealth.

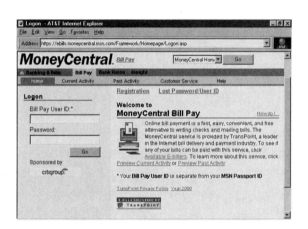

MoneyCentral offers a lot of basic information and updates on rates, but it also offers an online bill-payment service. This screen shot shows you the first page of its bill-payment system.

Credit Card Companies

Another new player venturing into banking is the credit card company American Express. In July 1999, American Express launched its online banking service, Membership B@nking (*www.membershipbanking.com*). This service offers competitive interest rates and reimburses ATM charges assessed by other banks.

The Ubiquitous Credit Card:

In the United States alone, American Express has 22 million charge card customers. The company is aiming for 1 million bank customers in five years. (*Online Banking Report*, July 1999)

On the home page of the service, there's a chart that makes it easy for you to locate the interest rates the company offers. We like the chart because it uses up-to-date numbers provided by *Bankinfo.com*. You should know that American Express is not just a credit card company anymore. It can provide you with money market investment products, savings and checking accounts, certificates of deposit, and lines of credit.

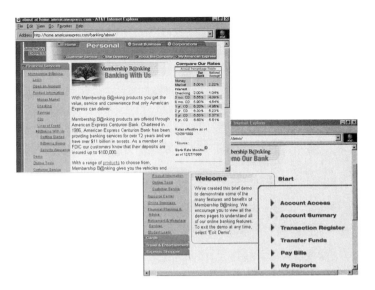

On the front page of its site, American Express Membership B@nking makes it easy for you to see its rates and to compare.

Membership B@nking has an easy site to navigate. On this demo page, the bank doesn't make you hunt around for the functions you will likely use regularly.

You Can Make Deals with Your Bank

We've painted this scenario of competition only to reinforce that you should be bartering with your bank. Tell your current bank about the better certificate of deposit rates you spot online or about the interest-bearing, free checking accounts. To keep your business, your current bank has to meet these offerings.

Who should you call? If there is a nearby branch, call or visit the branch manager. If you bank with an Internet-only institution, send an email to customer service and ask that a manager call you.

Smooth Surfing in Troubled Waters

We strongly recommend that you place calls to the management of your current bank if you are having problems or need to negotiate rates and fees. We also think you should avoid banking at institutions that don't have strong, user-friendly policies in place.

Internet banks have several features that can give you fair warning about their policies and give you a clear glimpse of how they work. If you use these tools before you sign up with a bank, you

Where Have All the Banks Gone?
In 1985, there were 14,417 banks and 3,626 thrifts or savings and loans in the United States. At the end of 1998, there were 8,774 banks and 1,728 thrifts. In just 14 years, 42 percent of all depository institutions disappeared. Consolidation was rampant in the 1990s.

will have a better understanding of the good and the bad you might encounter with the bank.

Visit the Physical Branch

Our first suggestion is helpful only if your Internet bank also has brick-and-mortar branches. If it does, visit your bank and try out the Internet site on their computers with a banker nearby. Many banks have demo computers for you to use in their lobbies so that you can test drive their systems. Some banks also hold one-night lectures on how to use their online services. Both of these learning vehicles are worth your time to make your online banking experience go smoothly from your first click.

Online Tools to Make the Banking Experience Better

If there is no actual bank to visit, there are many tools online that help you pick a bank or solve a problem. Use the features described in the following sections.

Frequently Asked Questions (FAQs)

FAQs are gold mines of information. As we were exploring dozens of sites, the FAQs are where we found some of the best information about the banks. Most of the time, you can find the FAQs for a site on the home page, but they can also be hidden behind customer information boxes or somewhere around the demos.

These lists of questions and answers can give you quick information. For example, if you can't find a rates button to learn what a bank charges, go to the FAQs page because that question will probably be answered there.

Firstar (*www.firstar.com*), based in Milwaukee, Wisconsin, has a FAQs list of about 10 questions and answers that give you the basic insights you need about a bank you are considering. The

FAQ page tells you about the security at the site, the equipment you will need to use the site, and other useful information.

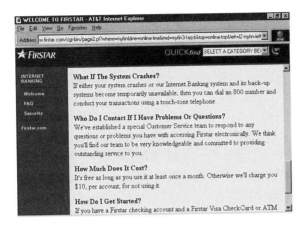

On the FAQ page of the Firstar site, you'll find questions and answers that can help save you money if you don't use the site at least once a month. Wow! That $10 charge could sting if you didn't know this information in advance.

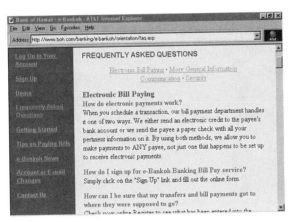

Bank of Hawaii (www.boh.com) has a FAQs link you can click on the first page of its online banking feature. The FAQs page lists answers to 15 questions, from how to pay bills online to tips on keeping your transactions secure.

Demonstrations

The demos are your next best source of information. In the real world, it's rare for your banker to give you a tour of the facilities. But in the virtual world, almost every Internet bank will take you on a tour of its site with a demo session.

Presidential Savings Bank, based in Bethesda, Maryland, has created a very helpful demonstration site that lets you quickly surf its Internet banking, bill payment, and statement viewing features. We like how the bank includes basic guidance next to the demo link buttons.

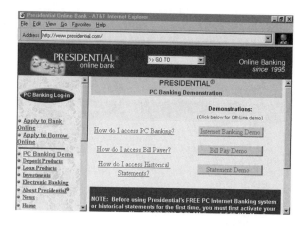

Ohio Savings Bank plays up its demo a little more than most banks. It has an animal character—a mouse named Webster—that will take you on a tour of the site.

24/7 Telephone Help

Although we've mentioned customer service help lines already, let us repeat that we consider this feature your best offline tool for your online banking. Some banks offer telephone access only during workday hours; others offer the service 24 hours a day, 7 days a week.

Because the beauty of online banking is the anytime, anywhere reality of it, we think you would be wise to pick a bank with 24-hour telephone access. That's the point of all of this. You want to bank at midnight, 3 a.m., or whenever you have the time.

THE BOTTOM LINE ON SANITY AND BANKING ONLINE

Some banks list their customer service telephone numbers on the first page of their sites; others place these phone numbers in the FAQs section or under a customer service or information click box.

In addition to their customer service by phone, banks also offer email assistance. Although we've found that banks are prompt in responding to emails, we still think that the phone service is the better route for instant information.

Site Directories

Site directories aren't unique to online bank sites, but most banks include them. It's a good way to learn what's there without all the interference from busy graphics. A site directory lists all the pages you can access, usually on one or a few screens, so that it only takes a quick glance to find what you want without having to click and click and click.

Bank United (www.bankunited.com), based in Houston, has a tab on its home page you can click for a site directory. When you open the directory, you'll find the list clear and to the point.

News Releases

Not all banks include news releases on their sites, but these articles can be very helpful as you try to learn more about your bank. The news releases are meant to give information to reporters, but consumers can use them to get the news directly from the institution.

Search Bars

As we were surfing hundreds of sites to do the research for this book, we sometimes found it nearly impossible to find what we wanted (like the site's demo or the FAQs). Luckily, some banks include *search bars* on their home pages. If you've been surfing around a site and are unsuccessful in finding what you want, try a search, if one is available.

You use the search bar in an intuitive manner: type the phrase you're looking for in the box and press Enter or click the Search or Find button next to the box. Most bank sites offer some tips on using their search function, so don't hesitate to use it if you're really stumped.

We know you are pressed for time and that scrolling through FAQs, reading news releases, and playing around with demos may at first seem like a waste time. Who likes to read the instructions anyway? When it comes to putting a ping-pong table together, you're right. You might be able to get by without reading the how-to booklet. But when it comes to Internet banking, we've found that the more you know, the better the experience, and the easier it is to get your banking accomplished.

Where to Go If Your Bank Fails You

If you do a lot of banking online or offline, you may run into problems when you feel you aren't being treated fairly at some point. Perhaps you signed up for a bill payment service, don't use it for a several months, and then discover that the bank is charging you for the service anyway. Because we are in a consumer's market, you might have a chance of getting those fees waived by calling the bank.

But sometimes you will have problems and your banker won't budge. This is when you should file complaints with state or federal banking regulators. At the least, you should contact the regulators to see whether they can offer assistance.

Keep the following list in mind when you need to take your complaint to someone who will care:

- *Federal Deposit Insurance Corporation*—Insurer of the majority of banks, Division of Compliance and Consumer Affairs, (800) 934-3342
- *Office of the Comptroller of the Currency*—For national banks, Customer Assistance Group, (800) 613-6743
- *Office of Thrift Supervision*—For thrifts or savings and loans, Consumer Program Division, (800) 842-6929
- *Board of Governors, Federal Reserve System*—Banks with state charters, Division of Consumer and Community Affairs, (202) 452-3667

Most of us don't know which of these agencies regulate our banks. To the consumer, it really doesn't matter until you have to file a complaint. For a quick online way to find out who regulates your institution, go to the *www.fdic.gov* site. There you can click Is My Bank Insured? And type in the name of your bank. If the bank is insured, the FDIC site will tell you which agency is the institution's primary regulator.

We also found the Federal Trade Commission Internet site (*www.ftc.gov*) to have helpful online advice. You can reach the FTC Consumer Response Center by phone at (877) FTC-HELP.

Bad, Bad Banks

We've tried to help you to find good banks online. But if you wind up with a dog of an online bank, you should know that you have plenty of other options. There is a site on the Internet, developed by an upset bank customer, that highlights complaints about banks online and off-line. The site is *www.badbanks.com*.

When we talked to the creator of BadBanks.com, he explained that he doesn't check on the complaints filed, but he does use some discretion and his instincts to determine which should be placed on his site.

The site keeper hears from bankers, too, griping about the complaints. This home page may be worth checking to see whether a bank you are considering as your financial institution has ended up with a complaint.

It looks official, but it's not. It's the Internet doing what it does best: providing a free forum for just about anyone to speak his or her mind about bad bank experiences.

What You Should Know Now

Don't be afraid to call your banker to complain, to ask for better service, or to negotiate a better rate. One of the hottest topics today for bankers is how they can retain their customers. That's you. Perhaps you can make a few suggestions.

Some of the best tools you can use as you learn to bank online are demos, frequently asked questions (FAQs), news releases, and site directories.

If you think your bank is treating you unfairly, take your complaint to the next level. Banking regulators want to hear from you.

CHAPTER 17

Welcome to the Future: What's Next for Online Banking?

Bankers are falling over each other—and every other Web player—as they race into the future. They want to be the ultimate Web host, better than Charles Schwab & Co., Yahoo!, Microsoft, eBay, and any of the other Internet-smart giants. A bank's competition comes in many forms in the online marketplace. It's not just other banks.

Banks know they must get online with more than static marketing pages and traditional financial service products. They've done that pretty well already. Take for instance, WingspanBank.com (*www.wingspan.com*), an Internet-only bank based in Wilmington, Delaware, established in 1999. This pure player, a bank without brick-and-mortar branches that is connected with its customers solely through Internet access, offers a wide array of financial products and management tools, including checking and savings accounts, mortgages, insurance products, and mutual fund investments. Today, a growing number of banks want to offer those products and more. They want to be the end-all, be-all love in your cyber world. You shouldn't have to go to any other site for your e-satisfaction. Whether it's for medical information, the weather, sports scores, insurance, investing, or buying certificates of deposits, banks want to be the key source of your e-xistence.

What You'll Learn in This Chapter:
- Why bankers are striving to be cyber-central.
- Smart appliances: How you can bank off your microwave oven.
- How online banking helps complete your e-life.

> **The Crystal Ball**
>
> Here are some predictions by a few of the top thinkers in the banking industry.
>
> Harvey Sax, president of HomeCom Communications: "Not too far in the future, consumers will log on to their community bank Web site and be greeted with a message addressing them personally such as 'Welcome back, Mr. Sax. It is good to hear from you again. Your last visit was on March 15, 2002.'"
>
> Matthew P. Lawlor, chairman and CEO of Online Resources & Communications Corporation: "The end of banking as we know it is not around the millennium corner, but there's no question that a new customer will dominate by 2020. She will rarely, if ever, set foot in a branch but will want instant access to her money and to move it in real-time."

There are primarily two ways bank CEOs will be able to achieve this unrequited relationship with us. They'll have to have smarter brains than other corporate executives, and their machines have to be smarter, too.

So what's next?

How Your Bank Plans to Woo and Wow You

Hopefully, this won't scare you: Banks plan to get into your brain. They want to market services and products to you that they already know you will want to buy. Mass-marketing to all six billion of us on planet Earth is definitely out. Customer-specific marketing is in. Each of us represents an individual market. We are no longer a part of a huge demographic group. With the ability of computers today to store and sort massive amounts of information, banks and other businesses are using data-mining techniques to increase their ability to understand who we are. This computer analysis allows a bank to predict with great precision the products and services we want to buy and exactly how much we are willing to spend to acquire those products.

Amazon.com is an expert in this one-on-one, highly-sophisticated marketing approach. When you buy a product from Amazon (*www.amazon.com*)—a book, for example—its system transfers a file into your computer's system. This sneaky file, called a *cookie*, tracks information about where you go on the host site and what interests you. With cookies, an e-business can customize messages to you each time you go to its domain. For example, if you buy a science book from Amazon.com, the next time you log on, the site will suggest other science-related publications. That's what happened to us when we bought a book about Rosalind Franklin, a woman scientist who took the first pictures of DNA.

Note how Amazon.com suggested that we might want to consider several titles related to DNA and science. The last book we bought was about DNA (don't ask), so why not offer us a few other titles on the same theme?

The players in e-commerce know that they must use technology tools such as cookies to stay in business. The Web world is cold, and we consumers will look for sellers who show at least a little care about who we really are—even if it isn't a human touch but a smart computer reaching out to us. The Internet is overwhelming to us as surfers and consumers. Thus, anyone who can filter it down to identify, in a non-intrusive fashion, what we really want is more likely to get our attention and business.

Banks and other e-commerce merchants may even have to give a little to their competitors if they want to become central points of contact for a consumer on the Web. The financial services industry likes to call this one-stop shop an aggregator. An *aggregator* collects information about all your commerce records and accounts, whether financial or not, and reports this data to you at one site. You may bank at Chase, fly with Delta, invest with Schwab, and have a couple of certificates of deposits at Citibank.

Even though these are separate companies, the smart bank—or for that matter, any aggressive e-commerce site—will want to enable you to get a report on all these accounts at their home page.

A banking software and systems provider, Edify, is already moving in this direction. The company is convincing its bank clients to become the aggregator of choice for its customers. BellSouth is one of the early users of this technology.

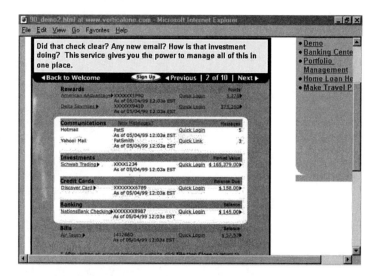

You can see that BellSouth is beating many e-sites in the race to become an information center for its customers. Here, with one master password, you can view your frequent flyer accounts for more than one airline, your investment account with Schwab, and your different email accounts.

Your One-Trick Computer Is Simply Outdated!

The future also brings with it the promise of a lot of cool, new hardware that will make online banking more convenient and far from what we knew in the late 1900s. What do you think about cooking a chicken in the microwave and reading your checking account balance at the same time off the door of the oven? NCR, which provides banks with computer systems, opened the Knowledge Lab, based in London, in 1996. The lab has developed a smart appliance—a microwave oven that can perform electronic banking functions while it heats up your dinner. The creators of the microwave bank figure that the kitchen is one of the most-used rooms in a home and that it would be a prime location to identify new Internet outlets. You are already there to cook and eat, so why not take a few moments to check on your savings account balance? The NCR microwave bank has been designed with a touch-screen monitor in the door and voice recognition software that eliminates the need for a keyboard.

The onslaught of other devices, many hand-held or that fit into your pocket, are also challenging the laptop and PC as the hardware of choice for banking online. Wireless connections to the Internet are gradually making hard-wired, bulky computers seem like unnecessary desk clutter. Palm Computing, Inc. has developed a hand-held platform that enables its users to access the Internet by simply raising a small antenna and dialing to the Web over the airwaves. Several models of cell phones have also evolved into Web phones, giving users access to the Internet over tiny, pocket-sized devices.

Both of these handy, hand-held devices keep you in touch with the cyber world, even if you are walking to lunch or rushing to and from meetings. As discussed in Chapter 11, "Trust Is More Than a Word," there is still a lot of product development necessary to combat the transfer of financial information over the Internet—especially over the airwaves.

The future will also bring with it a slew of new services and products offered by banks. Just last year, Congress and the president cleared the way for banks to more easily delve into the insurance and securities business. Along with making it easier to offer additional products, such as insurance and stocks, competition among online banks will force some banks to offer more novel products, services, and functions.

Bankinfo.com (*www.bankinfo.com*), an all-around source of banking information on the Web produced by Thomson Financial Publishing, asked its visitors what features they would like to see offered in the future as online banking grows and matures. The suggestions included providing customers with a personal finance program that would track their transactions (including noting what would be tax deductible); providing extranet sites that would allow a consumer to manage mortgages, auto, health, and home insurance, educational loans, and savings plans; offering customers free palm-held computers; providing free Internet access;

using real-time emails to alert customers about low checking account balances; and providing online chat sessions and online banking schools.

One of the more innovative suggestions from consumers was that banks should provide virtual-reality kiosks that would allow them to interact with the type of banker with which they are most comfortable (for example, a woman or a man, old or young, and perhaps even a dog). Bankinfo.com gladly reported that its survey showed that 85 percent of participants in its survey preferred banking with a golden retriever (a person's best friend).

Will All This Technology Drive Us Insane or to an E-asy Life?

The clock strikes 6 a.m. Your coffee maker clicks on and begins brewing your first cup of java. You rise to the morning news on your radio.

As you read the newspaper—yes, an old-fashioned paper version—you speak to your microwave bank. Recognizing your voice, the microwave begins summarizing the day's issues and events for you, including the status of your investment portfolio, what the markets are doing in other hemispheres, a reminder that today is the day to renew your certificates of deposit, an update on your checking and money market account balances, a suggestion to avoid the expressway on your way to work because of construction, a warning to wear a heavy coat to keep warm in the snow, and—by the way—congratulations, your favorite NFL team won in overtime after you went to bed.

Coming Soon:

The NCR Knowledge Lab has already developed this microwave bank. As the lab asserts, "Tomorrow's financial consumers will be as different as the technology they use. Today's 7-to-15-year-olds—the Wired Generation—will have no concept of a bank branch."

Before you take your last sip of coffee, your online bank makes one final suggestion: It's your mother's birthday and she likes red roses. You tell it to send a dozen ASAP. It shows you a picture of a bundle of roses and, through digital smell technology, you enjoy a whiff of the sweetness of your gift. When you are walking out to the car, you realize that any bank after the heart of your mother deserves all your business—whether it's as the vendor for your checking account or the purveyor of tickets to a Yankee's game. Your father's bank just won't ever be what it used to be.

What You Should Know Now

More and more, banks are adding several non-banking features to their sites to stay ahead of all of the competition on the Internet. They want to be your Web host. Don't be surprised when you can buy flowers from an Internet bank.

Get ready for banks to get inside your brain or at least into your home computer. They are dropping cookies into your hard drives. Cookie files track information about where you go on the host site. The banks want to customize marketing pitches to you based on your Web surfing.

In the future, will we do all of our banking on smart appliances in our homes and never set foot in a bank branch again? Yes, if banks can continue to improve their Internet sites by making them easier to navigate, faster, and free!

PART V
Appendixes

APPENDIX A

Banking Sites in This Book

Institution	URL	Comment
BankBoston	www.bankboston.com	Boston-based super-regional bank.
Bank of America	www.bankofamerica.com	Nationwide bank that has resulted from the merger of Nationsbank and Bank of America.
Bank of Hawaii	www.boh.com	Hawaii-based bank.
Bank of the West	www.bankofthewest.com	California-based provider of online banking services.
Bank One	www.bankone.com	A large nationwide bank and the backer of Wingspan Bank.
Bank United	www.bankunited.com	Houston-based bank.
Bay-Vanguard Federal Savings Bank	www.bayvanguard.com	An example of how a smaller community bank can effectively compete and serve customers through Internet-based online banking.
Busey Bank	www.busey.com	An Urbana, Illinois-based bank.

APPENDIX A

Institution	URL	Comment
Carolina First Bank	www.carolinafirst.com	South Carolina-based bank founded in 1986.
Centurion Bank	www.americanexpress.com/banking	American Express's bank and the home of its Internet Membership B@anking.
Chase Manhattan Bank	www.chasemanhattan.com	New York-based global bank.
Chittenden Bank	www.chittenden.com	Burlington, Vermont-based institution.
Citibank	wwww.citibank.com	New York-based global bank.
CompuBank	www.compubank.com	Another in a growing list of Internet-only banks or *pure players*.
Crestar Bank	www.crestar.com	A bank based in Richmond-Virginia.
Exchange Bank & Trust	www.ebankperry.net	Home of Exchange Bank & Trust of Perry, Oklahoma, on the World Wide Web.
First Internet Bank of Indiana	www.firstib.com	An Internet-only bank and the originator of the ad slogan "bank naked."
First National Bank & Trust of Pipestone	www.fnbpipe.com	Pipestone, Minnesota-based bank.
1st Source Bank	www.1stsource.com	Web site of 1st Source Bank of South Bend, Indiana.

Institution	URL	Comment
First Tennessee Bank	www.ftb.com	Based in Memphis, Tennessee.
First Union	www.firstunion.com	With BofA, one of the Charlotte, North Carolina-based heavyweights of banking.
Flagstar Bank	www.flagstar.com	Online banking provider based in Bloomfield Hills, Michigan.
GrandBank	www.grandbank-online.com	A Maryland-based bank.
Hibernia Bank	www.hibernia.com	Online banking in the Big Easy: Hibernia is based in New Orleans. Next challenge: virtual beignets and chicory-flavored coffee.
Key Bank	www.key.com	Owned by Cleveland-based KeyCorp.
Lyndonville Savings Bank	www.lyndonbank.com	A Vermont-based bank.
Net.B@ank	www.netbank.com	One of the new breed of Internet-only banks.
Ohio Savings Bank	www.ohiosavings.com	A Cleveland, Ohio-based institution with a speedy Web site.
Pennsylvania Business Bank	www.bizbank.org	A Philadelphia-based bank.
PNC Bank	www.pncbank.com	Pittsburgh-based bank.

Institution	URL	Comment
Presidential Savings Bank	*www.presidential.com*	Bethesda, Maryland-based bank.
Richmond County Savings Bank	*www.rcbk.com*	New Jersey-based bank.
Rocky Mountain Bank	*www.rmbank.com*	A Billings, Montana, bank that provides online banking services.
Salem Five Cents Savings Bank	*www.salemfive.com*	One of the first financial institutions to branch onto the Internet, Salem Five has expanded its Web presence to become even more of a full-service financial services provider through *www.direct-banking.com*.
Security First Network Bank	*www.sfnb.com*	The first bank to provide a full array of services from a site on the Internet.
Security One Federal Credit Union	*www.sofcu.org*	Membership includes anyone who lives, works, or worships in Arlington, Texas.
Stillwater National Bank & Trust Co.	*www.banksnb.com*	Online presence of Stillwater, Oklahoma, bank.
SunTrust	*www.suntrust.com*	Atlanta-based super-regional bank.

BANKING SITES IN THIS BOOK

Institution	URL	Comment
Telebank	www.telebank.com	Formerly a telephone banking powerhouse, Telebank has more recently shifted its focus to serving customers over the Internet.
United Bank	www.ubankal.com	Home of United Bank of Atmore, Alabama.
Wachovia Bank	www.wachovia.com	Based in Winston-Salem, North Carolina.
Walden Federal	www.waldenbank.com	A Walden, New York-based community bank.
Washington Mutual Savings Bank	www.washingtonmutual.com	The nation's largest savings institution is based in Seattle.
Wells Fargo Bank	www.wellsfargo.com	One of the first larger banks with a fully transactional Web site. Has successfully encouraged many customers to bank online.
Wingspan Bank	www.wingspanbank.com	The home of Bank One's Internet-only bank.
Zions Bank	www.zionsbank.com	A Salt Lake City, Utah-based bank.

Government Regulators and Agencies

Institution	URL	Comment
Federal Deposit Insurance Corp.	www.fdic.gov	Provides a wealth of information, including answering the question, "Is my bank insured?" as well as EDIE, the Electronic Deposit Insurance Estimator, which walks consumers through the process of calculating the adequacy of their deposit insurance coverage. A top-notch site.
Federal Financial Institutions Examination Council	www.ffiec.gov	An interagency group made up of the five bank and credit union regulatory agencies.
Federal Reserve Board of Governors	www.bog.frb.fed.us	The regulator of bank holding companies and member banks of the Federal Reserve System. Provides a host of economic information on this site as part of its role in setting economic and monetary policies.
Federal Trade Commission	www.ftc.gov	The Federal Trade Commission provides the Bureau of Consumer Protection and provides consumer information at its Web site.

Institution	URL	Comment
National Credit Union Administration	*www.ncua.gov*	Home of the agency charged with regulating and insuring federal and many state-chartered credit unions.
Office of the Comptroller of the Currency	*www.occ.treas.gov*	The OCC is a division of the Treasury Department and the regulator of national banks.
Office of Thrift Supervision	*www.ots.treas.gov*	Also a division of the Treasury Department, the OTS is the primary regulator of federally chartered savings institutions and savings and loan holding companies.
Securities Exchange Commission	*www.sec.gov*	The SEC is the regulator of stock exchanges and markets. Its Web site provides access to the filings of publicly listed companies through its EDGAR database.
Small Business Administration	*www.sba.gov*	A good source of information for starting or financing a small business, the SBA also maintains a site called U.S. Business Advisor at *www.business.gov*.

Institution	URL	Comment
U.S. Treasury Department	*www.treas.gov*	Home of the Treasury that oversees both the OCC and the OTS, which are financial institution regulatory agencies. The Treasury also markets savings bonds over the Internet through this site.

Helpful Reference Sites

Institution	URL	Comment
bankonline.com	*www.bankonline.com*	Provides a list of online banking providers around the world.
Bankrate.com	*www.bankrate.com*	Provides a variety of consumer information about banking.
Bankzip.com	*www.bankzip.com*	A one-stop source for information about finding a community bank in any region of the country.
Better Business Bureaus	*www.bbbonline.com*	A Better Business Bureau program focusing on e-commerce.
Gomez Advisors	*www.gomez.com*	A consumer information site and a consultant to online banks.

Institution	URL	Comment
National Fraud Internet Center	*www.fraud.org*	Established by the National Consumers League to address fraud in telemarketing.
Small Business Exchange	*www.americanexpress.com/small business*	A reference area of American Express's Web site that provides information for small business owners.

GLOSSARY

Altair Developed in 1974, the Altair was one of the first home computers.

applet A small browser-based program designed to do a specific job, typically written in a program language called *Java*.

automated clearing house (ACH) network A nationwide batch-oriented electronic payments system that provides for interbank clearing of transactions. The American Clearing House Association, the Federal Reserve, the Electronic Payments Network, and Visa act as ACH operators or clearing facilities through which financial institutions transmit or receive ACH payments.

bandwidth The transmission capacity of an electronic communications line, such as a communications network. The greater the bandwidth of a communications line, such as a telephone line or cable line, the higher the carrying capacity. Usually referred to in terms of bits per second.

Bankinfo.com All-around source for banking information on the Web produced by Thomson Financial Publishing.

Banking Information Technology Secretariat (BITS) The technology group for The Financial Services Roundtable created in 1996 to foster growth and development of electronic banking and commerce in an open environment.

Bankrate.com An online publication, *www.bankrate.com*, focusing on personal finance news and consumer information, including rate information from 4,000 financial institutions in more than 120 markets in the United States and Puerto Rico.

batch processing One system for how financial services institutions process customers' transactions and update their accounts in which many transactions are "batched," usually after a full day of business, before they are posted to individual accounts. In a real-time processing environment, transactions are posted to customers' accounts throughout the date. See also *real-time processing*.

BBBOnline A wholly-owned subsidiary of the Council of Better Business Bureaus with the mission to promote trust and confidence on the Internet through the BBBOnline Reliability and Privacy programs.

bill presentment The electronic delivery of bills either by the actual biller or by a financial services provider on behalf of the biller. This is the opposite of electronic bill payment.

bit A binary digit, 0 or 1, used in the representation of a number, letter, or special character. In most systems today, it takes eight bits (each containing a 1 or a 0) to represent a single character, such as the capital letter A.

baud Bits per second. This term is used to define the bandwidth of a communications line.

brick-and-mortar A term used to refer to offline businesses, bank branches, and corner stores, as opposed to an Internet bank or an e-commerce Web site. A trendy new term entering the banking lexicon is "click-and-mortar," an expression used to describe a bank serving customers through physical branches and through online banking services.

brochureware A static Web site that simply provides contact and marketing information but not transactional banking services.

browser A computer program that enables a personal computer user to retrieve information that has been made publicly available on the Internet. Netscape Navigator and Microsoft Internet Explorer are examples of browsers.

calculator A typical feature provided by financial institutions at their Web sites. A calculator allows customers to enter personal data to calculate loan terms, such as monthly payments and interest rates, as well as savings outcomes, such as what will it take to retire as a millionaire.

ciphertext   Encrypted text that appears as gibberish without the appropriate key to decode the message. See also *plaintext*.

consumer protection regulations   The Federal Reserve Board, among its authorities, develops rules to protect consumers including regulations B (equal credit opportunity); E (electronic funds transfer); M (consumer leasing); Z (truth in lending); CC (funds availability and collection of checks); and DD (truth in savings).

cookie   A file placed on your computer's hard drive by a Web site that you are visiting. This file allows the site being visited to log the pages you use and to determine if you have visited the site before.

credit bureaus   An agency that collects and distributes credit-history information of individuals and businesses. The three main credit bureaus are Equifax, Experian, and Trans Union.

credit scoring   A system used by banks and others to determine whether a customer is a good loan risk, taking into account your credit history including the number and type of accounts, bill-paying history, collection actions, late payments, and outstanding debt.

credit union   A cooperative organization chartered by a state or the federal government that accepts savings from its members and makes loans to its members. Credit unions are normally formed among members who are employed by the same company or are members of the same organization. Example: If you work at The White House, you can belong to the White House credit union.

cryptography   The principles, means, and methods for rendering information unintelligible and for restoring encrypted information to intelligible form.

decrypt   To unscramble a code. See also *ciphertext* and *plaintext*.

direct-dial   A computer-to-computer system of exchanging information. The first home banking systems were direct-dial, allowing consumers to use a computer with a modem to dial directly into the bank's computer system. The more popular method of home banking today is over the Internet (also called e-banking). With this method, bank customers connect or dial into the Internet and access their personal records by going to the bank's Web site, not directly to a computer system at the bank.

e-commerce The buying and selling of goods and services via the Internet. Also referred to as e-business. A provider of goods and services via the Internet may be called an e-tailer (rhymes with retailer).

EDIE (The Electronic Deposit Insurance Estimator) An online feature of the home page of the Federal Deposit Insurance Corp. EDIE is an online calculator that helps consumers determine the adequacy of their deposit insurance coverage at an FDIC-insured bank. See also *Federal Deposit Insurance Corporation*.

electronic bill payment A product or service offered by online financial services providers, such as banks, that allows you to pay bills from your computer via the Internet. The provider will either pay your bills electronically or by cutting a physical check and mailing it to the payee.

encryption The scrambling of data by a mathematical algorithm to prevent the understanding of the information absent an unscrambling code. The maximum level of encryption allowed in the United States is 128 bits.

ethernet A type of local area network originally developed by Xerox. Communication takes place by means of radio frequency signals carried over coaxial cable.

European Union EU, an institutional framework, created after World War II, for the construction of a united Europe designed to promote harmony among those nations.

FAQs Frequently asked questions. FAQs are featured on most Web sites as quick references for novice users of the site.

Federal Deposit Insurance Corporation (FDIC) Created in 1933 by Congress to restore public confidence in the nation's banking system by insuring deposits (*www.fdic.gov*).

Federal Financial Institutions Examination Council An interagency group made up of representatives of the five bank and credit union regulatory agencies. The FFIEC prescribes uniform principles, standards, and report forms for the federal examination of financial institutions and makes recommendations to promote uniformity among all of the federal bank and credit union regulatory agencies.

Federal Reserve System Made up of the Federal Reserve Board, the 12 regional Federal Reserve Banks, federally-chartered commercial banks and state-chartered commercial banks that elect to be members. The Federal Reserve System serves as a central credit facility for member commercial banks and controls the nation's money supply (*www.federalreserv.gov*).

Federal Trade Commission (FTC) The FTC enforces a variety of federal antitrust and consumer protection laws and seeks to ensure that the nation's markets function competitively and are vigorous, efficient, and free of undue restrictions. The agency also works to eliminate acts or practices that are unfair or deceptive.

Financecenter.com A cooperative venture that provides online personal finance tools.

financial services center A business that has developed into a one-stop-shop for financial products such as banking services, insurance, and stocks.

financial suite Software, such as Intuit's Quicken or Microsoft's Money, that allows you to manage your finances on your computer. Many are able to access information from Internet online banking sites.

firewall The combination of hardware and software that creates a boundary between two or more computer networks.

Gomez Advisors An e-commerce advisor to businesses and an online consumer information site (*www.gomez.com*). The organization is well-known for its online scorecards.

hacker An unauthorized user of a computer site. Also referred to as a cracker or vandal.

Hertz The frequency of electrical cycles per second. One Hertz equals one cycle per second. One MegaHertz (MHz) is equivalent to one million cycles per second. MHz is often seen as an expression of a personal computer's central processor, such as a 133 MHz CPU.

insufficient fund charges A fee assessed to a banking customer who fails to have adequate funds to cover transactions against a checking account. This is also known as an overdraft charge.

Internet bank   A bank that has established a presence on the World Wide Web to enable customers to perform certain functions, including viewing accounts and transferring funds. Some Internet banks are pure-players, meaning they only exist on the Web and have no brick-and-mortar branches. Similar terms include online bank, Web bank, and e-bank.

Internet Fraud Watch   A consumer online site run by the National Fraud Internet Center (*www.fraud.org*).

Internet Service Provider (ISP)   A company that provides access to the Internet, generally for a fee.

Internet Explorer   Microsoft's Web browser, often cited as a secure browser choice. Its major competitor is Netscape Navigator.

InterNetworking Group   Established in 1972 to bring standards to the Internet. The organization's first chairman was Vinton Cerf, who is considered the father of the Internet.

Intuit Incorporated   Developer of financial management software products, including Quicken, QuickBooks, and TurboTax.

Java   A compact, concise computer programming language, developed by Sun Microsystems. Java is perfect for the little applets that run on Web sites.

Jupiter Communications   Established in 1986 in New York, this organization provides research on Internet commerce.

key   A code that unscrambles encrypted data.

modem   A device that enables a computer to transmit data or information over an electronic communications line, such as a telephone line.

Money   Yes, it does make the world go around, but here we're referring to the personal financial management software produced by Microsoft.

MoneyCentral   Microsoft's comprehensive financial services page.

National Credit Union Administration   The federal agency that supervises and insures more than 6,700 federal credit unions and 4,100 state-chartered credit unions.

GLOSSARY

Netscape Communicator   A package of Web software products that includes the Web browser software Netscape Navigator.

Netscape Navigator   Web browser software, often cited as a secure choice. Its major competitor is Microsoft's Internet Explorer.

non-bank   A business that offers banking services, but as an adjunct to its core products and services.

Office of Comptroller of the Currency   Created in 1863, this bureau of the Treasury Department charters, regulates and examines national banks (*www.occ.treas.gov*).

Office of Thrift Supervision (OTS)   Established in 1989 as a bureau of the Department of Treasury, the OTS serves as the primary regulator of all federal and many state-chartered savings institutions (*www.ots.treas.gov*).

online bank   See *Internet bank.*

overdraft charge   See *insufficient fund charges.*

Personal identification number (PIN)   A PIN is often used as a password to obtain access to a secure portion of a Web site.

plaintext   A text message before it has been encrypted or after it has been decrypted or decoded. See also *ciphertext.*

portal   A Web site that offers access to the Web and an array of other services, including email and search engines.

privacy policy   A statement from an institution on how it will use the information it has gathered on you and whether it will sell your information to another company or use it to market products to you based on your personal profile. Privacy and the sharing of information about consumers is becoming a contentious issue among financial institutions, the government, and consumer groups.

proprietary systems   Computer software developed by banks so that customers could directly communicate with them and conduct banking transactions via a home computer equipped with a modem. See *direct-dial.*

pure-player   An Internet-only bank, one without brick-and-mortar branches.

Quicken   Personal financial management software produced by Intuit.

real-time processing   A transaction processing system in which bank transactions are posted to customers' account as they occur. See also *batch processing*.

remote banking   Banking transactions conducted apart from the physical premises of an institution, such as via the Internet, telephone, or a direct-dial system.

search engine   A software program capable of locating specified information or Web sites on the Internet. Examples are Yahoo!, AskJeeves, and Google.

Secure Sockets Layer (SSL)   A protocol for providing data security during transmission using data encryption, server authentication, and message integrity.

security   Broadly put, the protection of data against unauthorized access. Security can be ensured by several layers of technology, including firewalls and encryption, to protect the confidentiality of transactions over the Internet.

Small Business Administration (SBA)   Established in 1953, the SBA provides financial, technical, and management assistance to help Americans start, run, and grow their businesses (*www.sba.gov*).

snail mail   Mail delivered by the U.S. Postal Service or some other offline carrier.

sweep accounts   An account service provided by a bank in which a business' checking account funds are swept each night into an interest-bearing account. This system maneuvers around the prohibition of banks' paying interest on business accounts (Regulation Q).

teaser rate   An attractive offer by a credit card company that will last only for an introductory period before the interest rate rises significantly. Consumers should beware of these low rates that turn into far less competitive, higher rates.

TCP/IP   This acronym stands for transmission control protocol/Internet protocol, which makes possible communication via the Internet among different computers operating on different software platforms. The invention of TCP/IP is credited to Vinton Cerf and Bob Kahn.

terms and conditions   In online banking, a contract that includes the services, fees, rates, and guarantees associated with an institution and an account.

third-party provider   A company that provides a service on behalf of your bank or financial institution. In many cases, a bank's third-party relationship is transparent to consumers, meaning that the consumers think they are getting a particular service from their bank.

transactional site   A Web site where customers can perform functions, instead of just getting information. For example, a bank site offering customers the ability to view account histories, pay bills, transfer funds, and order checks is a transactional site.

Transport Layer Security (TLS)   A new Internet security protocol that is backward compatible with the SSL standard. See *Secure Sockets Layer*.

TravelersProperty Casualty   A company that provides remote banking insurance called SafeWeb and insures against unauthorized transactions in online accounts. CompuBank was one of the first online banks to provide this protection.

Truste   Founded in 1997, this is a privacy seal program offered by an independent organization dedicated to building consumer trust and confidence in the Internet (*www.truste.org*).

VeriSign   Founded in 1995, this organization provides public key infrastructure and digital certificate solutions to enable trusted commerce and communications over private and public networks.

World Wide Web   The WWW, or the Web, is actually a subnetwork of the Internet through which information is exchanged in text, graphic, audio, and video formats. World Wide Web is often used as a synonym for the Internet.

INDEX

Symbols

10 reasons to bank online, 14-16
128-bit encryption, 149-150
1st Source Bank (South Bend, Indiana) Web site, 63, 216
24-hour phone access (banking sites), 188, 200-201
40-bit encryption, 149

A

accounts
    analysis, 128
    downloading account information, 78-79
    fund transfers, 77-78
    opening online, 73-74
    registers, 54
    statements, 54
        viewing, 74-75
    transactions, viewing, 75
    viewing features, 23-24
accrued interest, 60
ACH (Automated Clearing House) network, 74, 89
Aetna Financial Services Web site, 19
aggregators, 207
Allen, Catherine, 136, 144-145
Altair, 10
Amazon.com Web site, 206
American Express
    Membership B@nking Web site, 196-197
    Small Business Exchange Web site, 130
amortization, 102
AOL's banking center, 57
applets (Java applets), 152
applying for loans, 55
ATMs (automation teller machines), 81
    foreign ATMs, 187
    location maps, 81
    rebates, 27, 187

B

BadBanks.com Web site, 203-204
bandwidth, 42
bank failures, 61-62
Bank of America Web site, 27, 39, 106, 122, 192, 215
Bank of Hawaii Web site, 199, 215
Bank of the West Web site, 123, 215
Bank One Web site, 191, 215
Bank Rate Monitor, 114
Bank United Web site, 201, 215
BankBoston Web site, 215
Bankinfo.com Web site, 196, 209
Banking Information Technology Secretariat (BITS), 136
banking regulators, filing complaints with, 202-203
banking sites, 198-202
    10 reasons to bank online, 14-16
    account statements, viewing, 74-75
    ATM location maps, 81
    batch processing, 78
    branch location maps, 80
    checks, ordering, 82
    cleared checks, viewing, 76
    community banks, 119
    connecting to, 40-42
    customer statistics, 14
    demos, 8
    download speed, 183
    downloading account information, 78-79
    email, sending, 82
    FDIC insured sites, finding, 62, 64-65
    features, 184-188, 197-202
        24-hour phone access, 188, 200-201
        ATM rebates, 187
        bill payment, 187
        demonstrations, 199
        FAQs (Frequently Asked Questions), 198-199
        free services, 186-187

news releases, 201
posted privacy policies, 185
real-time processing, 185
search bars, 202
site directories, 201
solid security systems, 184
fully-transactional sites, 12
fund transfers, 77-78
Gomez Advisors' Top 10 Internet Banks, 189-191
history of, 11-13
informational sites, 20
opening accounts, 73-74
privacy, 173-175
problem-solving, 202-203
real-time processing, 78, 183
risks of using, 32-33
security, *see* security
selecting, 47, 72
    broad searches, 48-50
    features to consider, 54-56
    focused searches, 50-54
    for business banking services, 127-128
    in-house demos, 53
SmartMoney's Top 10 Internet Banks, 189, 192
third-party technology providers, 137-138
transactional Web banking, 21-32
    24-hour access to real bankers, 30
    account viewing features, 23-24
    ATM rebates, 27
    brokerage services, 30
    certificates of deposit, 27
    credit card applications, 28
    custom Web pages, 25
    financial planning services, 28-29
    insurance sales options, 29
    interest-paying checking accounts, 26
    Internet access, 31
    mortgage applications, 27-28
    paying bills, 25
    shopping centers, 26
    software, interfacing with, 30
    tax information, 31
    transferring funds, 24
transactions, viewing, 75
user agreements, 73
user statistics, 83

bankonline.com Web site, 53, 222
Bankrate.com Web site, 72, 114, 116, 222
banks (traditional banks), decline of, 194, 197
Bankzip.com Web site, 119, 222
batch processing, 78, 185
baud (modems), 40
Bay-Vanguard Federal Savings Bank, 57-58
    Web site, 31, 51-52, 215
BBBOnline privacy seal, 164-165
Bernstein, Jodie, 160
Better Business Bureaus Web site, 222
    privacy seal programs, 168
bills, paying online, 25, 55, 85-95, 187
    Automated Clearing House (ACH) network, 89
    bill payment summaries, 90-91
    bill presentment, 93
    Chase Manhattan Bank Web site, 88
    Citibank Web site, 87, 90-91, 95
    CompuBank Web site, 94-95
    First Internet Bank of Indiana Web site, 89
    First Internet Bank Web site, 86
    First Tennessee Bank Web site, 95
    Flagstar Bank Web site, 94
    guarantees, 93
    Hibernia Bank Web site, 94
    non-sufficient funds, 89-90
    Ohio Savings Bank Web site, 86-87, 95
    overdraft protection, 89-90
    processing dates, 88-90
    site fees, comparing, 94-95
    Washington Mutual Savings Web site, 95
    Wells Fargo Web site, 86, 95
    Wingspan Bank Web site, 95
BITS (Banking Information Technology Secretariat), 136
    Financial Services Security Laboratory, 178
bits per second, 40, 42
bonds
    savings bonds, buying online, 108-109
    stocks and bonds, investing online, 105-106
branch location maps, 80
brokerage services, 30
Brown, Peter A., 142
browsers, secure browsers, 177

INDEX

brute force password cracking, 154
Bureau of Public Debt Web site, 109
Busey Bank Web site, 138-140, 215
business banking services, 121-126
    cash management, 124-125
    checking and savings accounts, 122-123
    comparing to consumer services, 126
    financing services, 121-122
    information resources, 130-131
    integrated banking, 123
    security issues, 128-129
    selecting online banks, 127-128
Business Gateway (Wells Fargo Bank Web site), 123
Busing, Lynn, 9
bytes per second (bandwidth), 42

C

Cable Modem Help Web site, 42
cable modems, 41-42
calculators (online calculators), 117-118
Carolina First Bank Web site, 216
cash management (business banking services), 124-125
Centurion Bank Web site, 216
Cerf, Vinton, 10
certificates of deposit, 27
Chase Manhattan Bank Web site, 81, 119, 216
    bill payment feature, 88
checking accounts
    business checking accounts, 122-123
    integrated banking, 123
    interest-paying checking accounts, 26
checks
    cleared checks, viewing, 76
    ordering online, 82
Chittenden Bank of Burlington Web site, 125
Chittenden Bank Web site, 216
ciphertext, 148
Citibank Web site, 7, 24, 73, 103-104, 191-192, 216
    bill payment feature, 87, 90-91, 95
cleared checks, viewing, 76
commercial banking, 128
community banks, 119
Compare Online Banks feature (Gomez Advisors Web site), 113

complaints, filing with banking regulators, 202-203
CompuBank Web site, 74-78, 167, 187-192, 216
    bill payment feature, 94-95
computers, 9-10
    future of online banking, 208-209
connecting to banking sites, 40-42
consumer protection regulations, 66-67
cookies, 175, 206
credit cards
    applying for, 28, 103-104
    teaser rates, 103
credit reporting agencies, 102-103
credit reports, 102-103
credit scoring, 98
credit unions
    insured credit unions, finding, 65
    loans, 98-99
    shares, 60
Crestar Bank Web site, 23-24, 192, 216
cryptography, 148-149
custom Web pages (banking sites), 25
customer relationship management, 159
customer statistics (online banking), 14
customer-specific marketing, 206-208

D

Data Encryption Standard (DES), 151
data security, 148
decline of the traditional bank, 194, 197
Deluxe Corp. Web site, 82
demographics of online bank customers, 14
demonstrations (banking sites), 8, 199
Department of Treasury Web site, 108
deposit insurance, 60-62
DES (Data Encryption Standard), 151
Diceware Web site, 153-154
Digital Insight, 83
direct-dial banking, 37
directories (site directories), 201
downloading
    account information, 78-79
    download speed, 183

E

e-commerce, 26
E-Loan Web site, 100-103
ebank.com Web site, 193

Electronic Deposit Insurance Estimator (EDIE), 60
electronic signatures, 73
email, sending through banking sites, 82
encryption, 9-10, 148-151
    128-bit encryption, 149-150
    40-bit encryption, 149
    Data Encryption Standard (DES), 151
    Enigma machine, 152
    public keys, 149
    secret keys, 149
    Secure Sockets Layer protocol (SSL), 149
    Transport Layer Security (TLS) protocol, 151
Enigma machine, 152
Equifax (credit bureau), 102
Exchange Bank & Trust Web site, 216
Exchange Bank of Perry, 20
Experian (credit bureau), 102

F

failed banks, 61-62
FAQs (Frequently Asked Questions), 198-199
FDIC (Federal Deposit Insurance Corporation), 60-65
    insured banking sites, finding, 62-65
    purchase and assumption, 61-62
    Web site, 61-65, 175-176, 203, 220
federal banking regulatory agencies, 65-66
Federal Financial Institutions Examination Council Web site, 66, 220
Federal Reserve, 65
    consumer protection regulations, 66-67
Federal Reserve Board of Governors Web site, 220
Federal Trade Commission, 66
    Web site, 203, 220
filing complaints with banking regulators, 202-203
Financenter.com Web site, 116
    online calculator, 117-118
financial management software, 42-45
financial planning services, 28-29
financial services modernization law, 162-163
financial suites, 35

financing services (business banking services), 121-122
finding
    insured banking sites, 62-65
    insured credit unions, 65
    online banks
        broad searches, 48-50
        focused searches, 50-54
firewalls, 9-10, 151
First Federal Savings Bank of Florida Web site, 21
First Internet Bank of Indiana Web site, 28, 47, 166, 189, 191, 216
    bill payment feature, 89
First Internet Bank Web site, 86
First National Bank & Trust of Pipestone Web site, 142, 216
First Tennessee Bank Web site, 217
    bill payment feature, 95
First Union Web site, 217
Firstar Web site, 198
Flagstar Bank Web site, 217
    bill payment feature, 94
float period, 188
foreign ATMs, 187
Forrester e-commerce consulting firm, 9
Frequently Asked Questions (FAQs), 198-199
FTC Consumer Response Center, 203
fully-transactional banking sites, 12
fund transfers, 77-78
future of online banking, 206-210
    computer hardware, 208-209
    customer-specific marketing, 206-208
    products and services, 209-210

G

General Accounting Office (GAO), 33
Gomez Advisors Web site, 72, 111-114, 183, 222
    Compare Online Banks feature, 113
    Internet Banker Scorecard, 112-113
Gomez Advisors' Top 10 Internet Banks, 189-191
Google.com Web site, 48, 152
government's role in online security, 144-145
GrandBank of Maryland Web site, 125
GrandBank Web site, 217

INDEX

H

hertz (bandwidth), 42
Hibernia Bank Web site, 217
    bill payment feature, 94
history of online banking, 11-13, 35-37
Huntington Web site, 191

I

identity theft, 161
informational sites, 20
Insurance Answer Center, The, 107
insurance sales options, 29
insurance, buying online, 107-108
insured banking sites, finding, 62-65
insured credit unions, finding, 65
integrated banking for businesses, 123
interest, accrued interest, 60
interest-paying checking accounts, 26
Internet
    development of, 10
    security, *See* security
Internet Banker Scorecard (Gomez Advisors Web site), 112-113
Internet service providers (ISPs), 31, 57-58
InterNetworking Group (INWG), 10
Intuit, 42-45
    Quicken, 43-44
investing in stocks and bonds online, 105-106
INWG (InterNetworking Group), 10
ISPs (Internet service providers), 31, 57-58

J-K

Java applets, 152
Jupiter Communications, 85

Key Bank Web site, 25, 192, 217
Komansky, David, 163

L

Lawlor, Matthew P. (CEO of Online Resources & Communications Corporation), 206
Little Orphan Annie, 140

loans, 98-103
    amortization, 102
    applying for, 55
    credit reports, 102-103
    credit scoring, 98
    E-Loan Web site, 100-103
    from online banks, 99-102
    from online credit unions, 98-99
    ZipDecision software, 98
lost passwords, 156
Lyndonville Savings Bank Web site, 138, 217

M

maps
    ATM locations, 81
    branch locations, 80
marketing, customer-specific marketing, 206-208
Mellon Bank Web site, 189
Membership B@nking Web site, 196-197
Microsoft, 42-45
microwave bank, 208
modems, 40-42
Money (Microsoft), 43-44
money market accounts, 54
MoneyCentral (MSN.com), 19, 43, 195-196
mortgage applications, 27-28

N

National Credit Union Administration (NCUA) Web site, 65-66, 221
National Fraud Information Center Web site, 178, 223
NCR Knowledge Lab, 208
Net.B@nk Web site, 13, 105, 191-192, 217
NetBank.com Web site, 56
news releases, 201
non-banks, 194-197
    Membership B@nking, 196-197
    MoneyCentral (MSN.com), 195-196
    PayMyBills.com, 195
non-sufficient funds (paying bills online), 89-90

O

Office of the Comptroller of the Currency, 62, 65
    risks of online banking, 32
    Web site, 65, 221
Office of Thrift Supervision Web site, 66, 221
Ohio Savings Bank Web site, 200, 217
    bill payment feature, 86-87, 95
one-way connections (cable modems), 41
online banking
    history of, 35-37
    learning about, 39
    over the Internet, 38
    personal financial management software, 38
    proprietary online services, 36
    proprietary software, 38
online banking sites, *see* banking sites
online calculators, 117-118
Online Privacy Alliance Web site, 165
opening accounts online, 73-74
ordering checks online, 82
overdraft protection, 89-90

P

Parsons, Ed, 42
passwords, 153-154
    brute force password cracking, 154
    Diceware Web site, 153-154
    lost passwords, 156
paying bills online, 25, 55, 85-95, 187
    Automated Clearing House (ACH) network, 89
    bill payment summaries, 90-91
    bill presentment, 93
    Chase Manhattan Bank Web site, 88
    Citibank Web site, 87, 90-91, 95
    CompuBank Web site, 94-95
    First Internet Bank of Indiana Web site, 89
    First Internet Bank Web site, 86
    First Tennessee Bank Web site, 95
    Flagstar Bank Web site, 94
    guarantees, 93
    Hibernia Bank Web site, 94
    non-sufficient funds, 89-90
    Ohio Savings Bank Web site, 86-87, 95
    overdraft protection, 89-90
    processing dates, 88-90
    site fees, comparing, 94-95
    Washington Mutual Savings Web site, 95
    Wells Fargo Web site, 86, 95
    Wingspan Bank Web site, 95
PayMyBills.com Web site, 195
PC banking, 38
PCs, 9-10
Pennsylvania Business Bank Web site, 126, 217
personal financial management software, 38, 42-43, 45
personalized Web pages (banking sites), 25
plaintext, 148
PNC Bank Web site, 108, 217
Polygraphiae libri ses ("Six Books of Polygraphy"), 149
portals to banking and finance, 56
Presidential Savings Bank Web site, 200, 218
privacy, 159-175
    10 privacy consumer tips, 173-175
    financial services modernization law, 162-163
    identity theft, 161
    industry standards, 160
    Online Privacy Alliance Web site, 165
    privacy policies, 164-165, 185
        CompuBank, 167
        First Internet Bank of Indiana, 166
        important components, 170-171
        Security First Network Bank, 165
        Wingspan Bank, 167
    privacy seals, 163-165, 168-169
        BBBOnline privacy seal, 164-165
        Better Business Bureau seal programs, 168
        TravelersProperty Casualty, 169
        Truste privacy seal, 168
        VeriSign, 169
processing dates (paying bills online), 88-90
proprietary online services, 36
proprietary software, 38

public keys (encryption), 149
purchase and assumption, 61-62
pure-play Internet banks, 26

Q-R

QuickBooks, 129
Quicken, 43-44
    Web site, 43, 79

Rackley, Tripp, 16
real-time processing, 78, 183-185
rebates (ATM rebates), 187
Regulation CC (consumer protection regulations), 67
Regulation E (consumer protection regulations), 67
Regulation Q, 125
regulators, filing complaints with, 202-203
regulatory agencies, 59
    FDIC (Federal Deposit Insurance Corporation), 60
    federal banking regulatory agencies, 65-66
    purchase and assumption, 61-62
Richmond County Savings Bank Web site, 129, 218
risks of online banking, 32-33
Rocky Mountain Bank Web site, 80, 99-100, 218
Roosevelt, Franklin D., 60

S

Salem Five Cents Savings Bank Web site, 188, 218
savings accounts, business savings accounts, 122-123
savings bonds, buying online, 108-109
Sax, Harvey (president of HomeCom Communications), 206
search bars, 202
searching
    insured banking sites, 62-65
    insured credit unions, 65
    online banks
        broad searches, 48-50
        focused searches, 50-54
secret keys (encryption), 149
secure browsers, 177
Secure Sockets Layer (SSL) protocol, 149
Securities Exchange Commission, 66
    Web site, 221

security, 136, 147-156, 175-178
    10 security consumer tips, 175-178
    bank site explanations of security, 138-142
    business banking services, 128-129
    consumer responsibility, 145-146
    cryptography, 148-149
    data security, 148
    encryption, 9-10, 148-151
        128-bit encryption, 149-150
        40-bit encryption, 149
        Data Encryption Standard (DES), 151
        Enigma machine, 152
        public keys, 149
        secret keys, 149
        Secure Sockets Layer (SSL) protocol, 149
        Transport Layer Security (TLS) protocol, 151
    firewalls, 9-10, 151
    government's role in online security, 144-145
    passwords, 153-154
        brute force password cracking, 154
        Diceware Web site, 153-154
        lost passwords, 156
    protective measures taken by online banks, 142-144
    security systems, 184
    steps to protect security, 155-156
    third-party technology providers, 137-138
Security First Network Bank Web site, 12, 36, 165, 190-192, 218
Security One Federal Credit Union Web site, 99, 218
selecting online banks, 47
    features to consider, 54-56
    in-house demos, 53
    search process
        broad searches, 48-50
        focused searches, 50-54
sending email through banking sites, 82
servers, 149
shares, 60
shopping centers (banking sites), 26
shopping malls (virtual shopping malls), 118-119
site directories, 201
Small Business Administration Web site, 130, 221

small business banking services, 121-126
    cash management, 124-125
    checking and savings accounts, 122-123
    comparing to consumer services, 126
    financing services, 121-122
    information resources, 130-131
    integrated banking, 123
    security issues, 128-129
    selecting online banks, 127-128
Small Business Exchange Web site, 130, 223
SmartMoney's Top 10 Internet Banks, 189, 192
software
    personal financial management software, 38, 42-45
    proprietary software, 38
speed (download speed), 183
SSL (Secure Sockets Layer) protocol, 149
static Web pages, 20
statistics of online bank customers, 14
Steganographia ("Covered Writing"), 149
steganography, 150
Stillwater National Bank & Trust Company Web site, 139-141, 218
stocks and bonds, investing online, 105-106
SunTrust Bank Web site, 129, 218
sweep accounts, 121

T

tax information, 31
teaser rates (credit cards), 103
technology, 8-11
    Internet, development of, 10
    PCs, 9-10
    security developments, 10
technology providers, 137-138
Telebank Web site, 22, 29, 100-102, 107, 192, 219
telephone help (banking sites), 200-201
telephone modems, 40
third-party technology providers, 137-138
thrifts, 99
Tinker Federal Credit Union Web site, 82
TLS (Transport Layer Security) protocol, 151
traditional banks, decline of, 194, 197

Trans-Union (credit bureau), 102
transactional sites, 186
transactional Web banking, 21-32
    24-hour access to real bankers, 30
    account viewing features, 23-24
    ATM rebates, 27
    brokerage services, 30
    certificates of deposit, 27
    credit card applications, 28
    custom Web pages, 25
    financial planning services, 28-29
    insurance sales options, 29
    interest-paying checking accounts, 26
    Internet access, 31
    mortgage applications, 27-28
    paying bills, 25
    shopping centers, 26
    software, interfacing with, 30
    tax information, 31
    transferring funds, 24
transactions, viewing, 75
transferring funds, 24, 77-78
Transport Layer Security (TLS) protocol, 151
TravelersProperty Casualty privacy seal, 169
Treasury Department Web site, 222
Trithemius, Johannes, 149-150
trust, 135
Truste privacy seal, 168
two-way connections (cable modems), 41

U-V

U.S. Business Advisor Web site, 130
U.S. Department of Treasury Web site, 108
U.S. General Accounting Office (GAO), 33
U.S Treasury Department Web site, 222
United Bank Web site, 21, 219
US Access Bank Web site, 191
USAccess Web site, 192
user agreements, 73
user statistics (online banking), 83

VeriSign privacy seal, 169
virtual shopping malls, 118-119

W

Wachovia Web site, 7, 28, 192, 219
Walden Federal Web site, 186, 219
Washington Mutual Savings Bank Web site, 28, 219
　　bill payment feature, 95
Web browsers, secure browsers, 177
Web sites
　　First Union, 217
　　1st Source Bank (South Bend, Indiana), 63, 216
　　Aetna Financial Services, 19
　　Amazon.com, 206
　　American Express Small Business Exchange, 130
　　BadBanks.com, 203-204
　　Bank of America, 27, 39, 106, 122, 192, 215
　　Bank of Hawaii, 199, 215
　　Bank of the West, 123, 215
　　Bank One, 191, 215
　　Bank United, 201, 215
　　BankBoston, 215
　　Bankinfo.com, 196, 209
　　bankonline.com, 53, 222
　　Bankrate.com, 72, 114, 116, 222
　　Bankzip.com, 119, 222
　　Bay-Vanguard Federal Savings Bank, 31, 51-52, 215
　　Better Business Bureau, 222
　　　　privacy seal programs, 168
　　Bureau of Public Debt, 109
　　Busey Bank, 138-140, 215
　　Cable Modem Help, 42
　　Carolina First Bank, 216
　　Centurion Bank, 216
　　Chase Manhattan Bank, 81, 119, 216
　　　　bill payment feature, 88
　　Chittenden Bank, 216
　　Chittenden Bank of Burlington, 125
　　Citibank, 7, 24, 73, 103-104, 191-192, 216
　　　　bill payment feature, 87, 90-91, 95
　　CompuBank, 74-78, 167, 187-192, 216
　　　　bill payment feature, 94-95
　　Crestar Bank, 23-24, 192, 216
　　Deluxe Corp., 82
　　Department of Treasury, 108
　　Diceware, 153-154
　　E-Loan, 100-103
　　ebank.com, 193
　　Exchange Bank & Trust, 216
　　FDIC (Federal Deposit Insurance Corporation), 61-65, 175-176, 203, 220
　　　　checking insured banks, 63
　　　　finding insured banks, 65
　　Federal Financial Institutions Examination Council, 66, 220
　　Federal Reserve, 65
　　Federal Reserve Board of Governors, 220
　　Federal Trade Commission, 203, 220
　　Financenter.com, 116-118
　　First Federal Savings Bank of Florida, 21
　　First Internet Bank, 86
　　First Internet Bank of Indiana, 28, 47, 166, 189, 191, 216
　　　　bill payment feature, 89
　　First National Bank & Trust of Pipestone, 142, 216
　　First Tennessee Bank, 217
　　　　bill payment feature, 95
　　Firstar, 198
　　Flagstar Bank, 217
　　　　bill payment feature, 94
　　Gomez Advisors, 72, 111-114, 183, 222
　　　　Compare Online Banks feature, 113
　　　　Internet Banker Scorecard, 112-113
　　Google.com, 48, 152
　　GrandBank, 217
　　GrandBank of Maryland, 125
　　Hibernia Bank, 217
　　　　bill payment feature, 94
　　Huntington, 191
　　Key Bank, 25, 192, 217
　　Lyndonville Savings Bank, 138, 217
　　Mellon Bank, 189
　　Membership B@nking, 196-197
　　MSN.com MoneyCentral, 19, 43, 195-196
　　National Credit Union Administration, 66, 221
　　National Fraud Information Center, 178, 223
　　Nct.B@nk, 13, 105, 191-192, 217
　　NetBank.com, 56
　　Office of the Comptroller of the Currency, 65, 221

Office of Thrift Supervision, 66, 221
Ohio Savings Bank, 200, 217
    bill payment feature,
      86-87, 95
Online Privacy Alliance, 165
PayMyBills.com, 195
Pennsylvania Business Bank,
    126, 217
PNC Bank, 108, 217
Presidential Savings Bank, 200, 218
Quicken, 43, 79
Richmond County Savings Bank,
    129, 218
Rocky Mountain Bank,
    80, 99-100, 218
Salem Five Cents Savings Bank,
    188, 218
Securities Exchange Commission,
    221
Security First Network Bank, 12, 36,
    165, 190-192, 218
Security One Federal Credit Union,
    99, 218
Small Business Administration,
    130, 221
Small Business Exchange, 223
Stillwater National Bank & Trust
    Company, 139-141, 218
SunTrust Bank, 129, 218
Telebank, 22, 29, 100-102, 107,
    192, 219
Tinker Federal Credit Union, 82
U.S. Business Advisor, 130
U.S. Treasury Department, 222
United Bank, 21, 219
US Access Bank, 191
USAccess, 192
Wachovia, 7, 28, 192, 219
Walden Federal, 186, 219
Washington Mutual Savings Bank,
    28, 219
        bill payment feature, 95
Wells Fargo Bank, 12, 123, 145,
    177, 184, 191-192, 219
        bill payment feature, 86, 95
        Business Gateway, 123
Wingspan Bank, 25, 29, 73, 105,
    167, 187, 191, 205, 219
        bill payment feature, 95
Zions Bank, 122, 219

X-Z

Yahoo's banking page, 57

Zions Bank Web site, 122, 219
ZipDecision software, 98

Sams Teach Yourself e-Travel Today

Planning Vacations, Finding Bargains, and Booking Reservations Online

Mark Orwoll
ISBN: 0-672-31822-9
$17.99 US/$26.95 CAN

Other Sams Teach Yourself Today Titles

e-Trading
Tiernan Ray
ISBN: 0-672-31821-0
$17.99 US/$26.95 CAN

e-Personal Finance
Ken and Daria Dolan
ISBN: 0-672-31879-2
$17.99 US/$26.95 CAN

e-Music
Brandon Barber
ISBN: 0-672-31855-5
$17.99 US/$26.95 CAN

e-Banking
Mary Dixon and
Brian Nixon
ISBN: 0-672-31882-2
$17.99 US/$26.95 CAN

e-Job Hunting
Eric Schlesinger and
Susan Musich
ISBN: 0-672-31817-2
$17.99 US/$26.95 CAN

e-Parenting
Evelyn and Karin
Petersen
ISBN: 0-672-31818-0
$17.99 US/$26.95 CAN

All prices are subject to change.

SAMS

www.samspublishing.com

Tell Us What You Think!

As the reader of this book, *you* are our most important critic and commentator. We value your opinion and want to know what we're doing right, what we could do better, what areas you'd like to see us publish in, and any other words of wisdom you're willing to pass our way.

As an Associate Publisher for Sams, I welcome your comments. You can fax, email, or write me directly to let me know what you did or didn't like about this book—as well as what we can do to make our books stronger.

Please note that I cannot help you with technical problems related to the topic of this book, and that due to the high volume of mail I receive, I might not be able to reply to every message.

When you write, please be sure to include this book's title and author as well as your name and phone or fax number. I will carefully review your comments and share them with the author and editors who worked on the book.

    Fax: 317-581-4770

    Email: *internet_sams@mcp.com*

    Mail: Mark Taber
                Associate Publisher
                201 West 103rd Street
                Indianapolis, IN 46290 USA